THE WORKS OF WILLIAM H. BEVERIDGE

Volume 2

THE PILLARS OF SECURITY

THE PILLARS OF SECURITY
And Other War-Time Essays and Addresses

SIR WILLIAM H. BEVERIDGE

Routledge
Taylor & Francis Group

LONDON AND NEW YORK

First published in 1943

This edition first published in 2015
by Routledge
2 Park Square, Milton Park, Abingdon, Oxon, OX14 4RN

and by Routledge
711 Third Avenue, New York, NY 10017

Routledge is an imprint of the Taylor & Francis Group, an informa business

British Library Cataloguing in Publication Data
A catalogue record for this book is available from the British Library

ISBN: 978-1-138-82643-4 (Set)
eISBN: 978-1-315-73730-0 (Set)
ISBN: 978-1-138-82823-0 (Volume 2)
eISBN: 978-1-315-73822-2 (Volume 2)

Publisher's Note
The publisher has gone to great lengths to ensure the quality of this reprint but points out that some imperfections in the original copies may be apparent.

Disclaimer
The publisher has made every effort to trace copyright holders and would welcome correspondence from those they have been unable to trace.

THE
PILLARS OF SECURITY

AND OTHER WAR-TIME ESSAYS AND ADDRESSES

By

Sir William H. Beveridge, K.C.B., F.B.A.

*'The art of leadership is making common men do
uncommon things.'—Unpublished Report*

LONDON
GEORGE ALLEN & UNWIN LTD.
MUSEUM STREET

BOOK
PRODUCTION
WAR ECONOMY
STANDARD

PRINTED IN GREAT BRITAIN
in 11-Point Garamond Type
BY UNWIN BROTHERS LIMITED
WOKING

CONTENTS

ILLUSTRATIONS

AN ECONOMIST REPORTS

Reproduced by permission of the Proprietors of the "Evening Standard"
(See Note 1)

INTRODUCTION

THE nineteen papers which form this volume were prepared separately for different occasions between the beginning of February, 1942, and the end of March, 1943. Some duplication of thought and phrase between them is inevitable, though I have reduced this as much as possible by judicious selection. I hope that the papers, in spite of their diverse origins, will be found to have a substantial unity. They are nearly all variations on two complementary themes: that war and peace for a democracy are indivisible and that war-time requires methods of government different from those of peace-time.

Of these two themes the first is the principal one, but it does not enter at the outset. The earliest papers, appearing when the fortunes of the United Nations seemed to be at their lowest ebb in the first quarter of 1942, are concerned with the conditions and methods of making the immediate war effort of Britain more total and more effective. Their theme is the secondary one of the need for differences in the machine and spirit of Government between peace-time and war-time. At the time of their preparation, I was still fresh from the Report of the Committee on Skilled Men in the Services and about to embark on Fuel Rationing. These official tasks are not the subject of any of the papers in this volume, but are illustrated here by two of Mr. Low's most engaging cartoons and are described briefly in the Chronological and other Notes.

The principal theme appears for the first time in the fifth paper, representing an address on Maintenance of Employment which I gave in July, 1942. I was then far advanced in preparation of my Report on Social Insurance and Allied Services and from the evidence presented to my Committee had already begun to realize what I described later as "one of the discoveries of the year 1942," namely, the deep and vivid interest of the people of Britain in the kind of Britain which is to emerge when the floods of war subside. This interest was made patent to all by the reception accorded to the Report on Social Insurance and Allied Services which I signed on the 20th November, 1942, and which was published on the 1st December following.

The present collection of papers enables me in two ways to put that Report more clearly in its proper perspective. First, the Plan for Social Security proposed by me is described in the Report itself as part of a comprehensive programme of social reform directed to deal not only with Want but with the four other giant evils of Disease, Ignorance, Squalor and Idleness. It would have been inappropriate to develop this aspect of my proposals more fully in the Report itself, but it is emphasized in many of the papers appearing in this volume and particularly in the address which I gave at Oxford immediately after the publication of the Report, outlining in general terms a programme of "New Britain."

Second, the Plan for Social Security is presented in one of the closing paragraphs of my Report as a contribution towards success in war, by securing from the British people their maximum of effort:—

> There is no need to spend words today in emphasizing the urgency or the difficulty of the task that faces the British people and their Allies. Only by surviving victoriously in the present struggle can they enable freedom and happiness and kindliness to survive in the world. Only by obtaining from every citizen his maximum of effort, concentrated upon the purposes of war, can they hope for early victory. This does not alter three facts: that the purpose of victory is to live into a better world than the old world; that each individual citizen is more likely to concentrate upon his war effort if he feels that his Govern-

ment will be ready in time with plans for that better world; that, if these plans are to be ready in time, they must be made now.*

This aspect, also, of my Plan it would have been inappropriate to develop at any length in the Report itself, but it finds repeated expression in a number of the papers in this volume. It is summed up in a phrase which I used on more than one occasion in the last few months, but have left standing only in one of the papers as here printed; that democracies, like Cromwell's armies, need to know what they fight for and to love what they know.

I have described the deep interest of the British people during war in what should happen after war as one of the discoveries of 1942. Not only the discovery, but the fact of this interest is new. There was no equal interest in post-war problems during the first World War. My Report on Social Insurance, had it been made in that war, would almost certainly have met with a very different reception. To that I can speak from personal experience.

In the first World War I was a Civil Servant engaged nearly continuously on one or other of the novel problems of the home front, presented by what was then the unprecedented phenomenon of total war. Though in contrast to my experience in the present war, I found myself engaged almost wholly on immediate tasks of war, it fell to me occasionally to look forward to the peace. One such occasion was in the summer of 1916 when it seemed worth while to the Government of the day to commission a few officials in the Board of Trade to consider the industrial problems that would arise when the war ended. The first fruit of that consideration was the introduction of a Bill to extend the scheme of unemployment insurance, established in 1911 for engineering, shipbuilding, building and a few other trades, to a much larger body of workpeople including munition workers generally. The fate of this

* *Report on Social Insurance and Allied Services*, para. 458.

attempt at post-war planning, as described by myself some years ago is instructive:—

> This measure had a curious history. It passed through both Houses of Parliament without opposition and practically without comment, and became law on 4th September, 1916. Then the difficulties began. The authors of the Act had in view at the end of the war a general dislocation of industry and the need for practically universal insurance; they framed a measure which under the guise of insuring munition workers brought in the whole of many trades and might have been extended by order to practically every trade, for no trade was without some munition work. The House of Commons in 1916 was little interested in what would happen if and when the war ended. The employers and workpeople engrossed in prosperity would not look beyond their noses. The extension of insurance so light-heartedly voted by Parliament met with vigorous and successful resistance by one trade after another. . . . The line taken was that the trades had unfilled orders enough to keep them busy for years after the war, and that if they did have unemployment they could provide for it much better by themselves than under the State scheme. None of the trades in fact made any serious attempt to frame schemes of their own; employers and workpeople were content to unite in purely negative opposition to officials and the State. . . . The net result of the new Act was to bring into insurance 1,100,000 persons, of whom about three-quarters were women and girls.*

The defeat of this first attempt to give economic security after the first World War was complete. The difference between the reception accorded by the public to that

* *War and Insurance*, pp. 232-3 (Carnegie Endowment Economic and Social History of the World War, 1927).

attempt and the response accorded to my recent Report shows the depth of the gulf which separates us today from the world of twenty-five or thirty years ago. The gulf is made by the bitter experience of the interval between the two wars.

During the first World War it seemed to the mass of the people unimportant to plan the peace. After the war had ended they might expect to go back to the good old pre-war days with fair contentment. Today there is no such prospect of contentment in going back, because the times before the second World War were not good. The British people have learned by experience that after this war they must go forward to something new, not back to the old. As sensible people, they realize that one goes forward better if one has looked ahead and has made plans for the journey.

I had a second experience of planning reconstruction during the first World War which also has its moral for today. This was in the month of February, 1918, when the war was beginning to rise to its military climax. That was a month of crisis also in the Ministry of Food, where Stephen Tallents and I were preparing the London and Home Counties rationing scheme to deal with the food queues—probably as absorbing a time of anxious work as either of us ever experienced. Yet that was also the month when the Report of a Reconstruction Sub-Committee on Unemployment Insurance, of which I was Chairman, reached its final stages and was completed. The Report pointed to the prospect of widespread industrial dislocation after the war and urged the generalization of unemployment insurance: "Unless a scheme of general insurance is devised and launched at the earliest possible date it may be impossible to avoid the disastrous chaos of unorganized and improvised methods of relieving distress."

The Minister specially charged with Reconstruction in those days had no stronger position than his successor today and no steam of public opinion behind him. The

Report of my Sub-Committee, signed on 12th February, 1918, was unanimously approved a month later by the main Committee on Civil War workers and then fell into doldrums. A spell of inter-departmental battledore and shuttlecock ended half-way through 1919 in the appointment of a committee of officials to frame a scheme, which led ultimately to the generalization of insurance in 1920 about two and a half years after the original Report. In the meantime the nation had duly descended into the chaos of unorganized and improvised relief forecast by the Report.

This second experience of the last war is cited here to suggest: first, that it is not impossible simultaneously to conduct war and to make plans for peace; second, that decision on the plans when framed depends on the strength of the machinery of Government at its top.

The second World War has brought us on more than one occasion into greater perils than we have experienced in the first World War: it calls unquestionably for the maximum of individual effort from every person in the community, directed in the first instance to the aim of victory in war. For the individual, war must be total, in the sense that every individual must do with all his strength that which he is asked to do as his war job. For the Government of the British democracy, its war job includes planning for peace; giving assurance to the citizens that it is planning courageously, imaginatively, justly and in good time; securing thereby from each citizen his whole-hearted concentration upon whatever task may be assigned to him. The war Government of a democracy must be strong enough at the top to conduct war and to plan peace simultaneously. In the two chapters that end this volume, its principal theme and its secondary theme unite.

A postscript, added at the last moment, shows economic security in its setting of larger problems.

W. H. BEVERIDGE.

MASTER'S LODGINGS,
UNIVERSITY COLLEGE, OXFORD.   *11th April,* 1943.

GOVERNMENT FOR WAR: A COMPARISON WITH 1916-18*

THE immediate outcome of the recent Parliamentary debate on the conduct of the war has been the appointment of Lord Beaverbrook as Minister of War Production, with a reshuffle of subordinate posts.† Such an appointment is not in form a step nearer to the kind of war Government established in December, 1916. Whether it can be made so in substance and can help to bring such a Government into being rapidly is perhaps the most vital issue before the nation and its leaders today.

The requisites for success in war government are three-fold: speed of executive action, correctness and speed of decision on policy, and that the nation should understand and support the actions of the Government. The first requirement is satisfied in proportion as responsibilities for executive action are clearly defined and all those responsibilities which hang closely together by nature are closely associated in the departmental structure. The second requirement involves the taking of decisions neither by one man nor by a committee of hurried executives, but by a group of men pooling their minds in constant session —men freed from daily executive tasks so that they have time to think before they decide, men with unquestioned authority over all departmental Ministers, so that what they decide is a decision, not a time-wasting compromise. The third requirement involves putting in charge of each Department a named Minister directly responsible to Parliament which represents the nation.

Some may question whether the third requirement is

* *The Times*, 16th February, 1942.   † See Note 2.

essential for success in war or is essential only for success by a democracy. My answer is that the one solid hope for the success of Britain in this war is the fact that Britain is a democracy allied to democracies: that the conflict is between the British people and their enemies, not between individual leaders; that by consequence the British people cannot be beaten by any psychological weakness or till they are physically helpless.

The form of Government established at the end of 1916 was consciously designed to satisfy the three requirements of success in war as set out above. Executive action was entrusted to departmental Ministers directly responsible to Parliament; they could proceed and were encouraged to proceed with full speed in their own spheres. They had above them a War Cabinet of Ministers without Portfolio, in nearly constant session, able at once to give a decision on any issue of major policy or any point of clash between Departments. It was possible and natural for one member of the War Cabinet to pay special attention to a particular group of topics, such as defence or munitions production or imperial relations. When any such problem came before them, his colleagues would expect him to have mastered all the relevant documents, even if they had not done so themselves; he might be asked by the Cabinet personally to settle, after inquiry, some special issue. Lord Milner, for example, became to a large extent the specialist of the 1917 Cabinet on many home front issues. But because he was Minister without Portfolio he neither interfered with the direct responsibility of each departmental Minister nor was he expected by Parliament to answer questions. That was the duty of the departmental Minister.

It is said sometimes that Ministers without Portfolio, lacking intimate contact with administration, will be too remote and too ignorant to be able to give sound judgments or to impose their will upon powerful executive Departments. The main answer to this objection depends upon choosing the right men for the War Cabinet. The subsidiary answer is that these men need not lack knowledge or expert assistance. The War Cabinet should not duplicate the work of the Departments, but it can have its own secretariat for economics, defence, and other groups of problems, to ensure that the wider implications of every proposal coming before the War Cabinet have been studied.

It is said also by some that the War Cabinet of 1916-18 was small in appearance only, since its actual meetings were attended by numerous other Ministers and their officials. This is true of some meetings though not of all; when a question affecting any Department (practically every question was bound to affect some Department) was before the War Cabinet, the Ministers concerned were summoned and they sometimes brought their principal officials. But this no more made the War Cabinet itself into a large body than the presence of counsel, solicitors, and others in the Court of Appeal makes the Court itself anything but a small body. The War Cabinet of 1916-18 had the unquestioned authority of judges and the same detachment from detail. The departmental Ministers were there only to put their particular case and answer questions. The decision was that of the War Cabinet given then or later, not by compromise but by judgment.

The Governments which have conducted this war for Britain hitherto have borne no likeness to the Government which conducted us to victory in 1918. In the present Government all the dominant personalities, from the Prime Minister downwards, have been eagerly absorbed in executive tasks; there are some Ministers without Portfolio but they have been made recessive. What difference to the contrast between the last war and this war is made by the new appointment of a Minister of Production? The answer depends to some extent upon the functions and way of work of the new Minister.

On the face of it appointment of a Minister of Production is neither a step towards the War Cabinet model of 1916–18 nor a step away from it. It is a move on a different plane, in the direction of grouping Departments and setting up a super-Minister for that group. The demand for a Minister of Production has sprung from a desire to secure greater co-ordination between the different branches and factors of production. Many of those who have made the demand have clearly had in mind a return to something like the Ministry of Munitions which, in the last war, covered most of the ground now occupied by the Ministry of Supply and the Ministry of Aircraft Production, and had its own Labour Department.

There were great advantages in this combination then. But there are serious difficulties in the way of such departmental combination today. Production depends in the last resort upon man-power; a Ministry of Production without authority over labour is a contradiction in terms. In the last war there was no Ministry of Labour till long after the Ministry of Munitions with its Labour Department had been firmly established. In the present war the Ministry of Labour has held a key position from the beginning; it has additional functions of national service which fall outside the sphere of munitions production and fell to another Department in 1914–18. Apart from any question of Ministerial personalities, an attempt to re-create the Ministry of Munitions for this war is out of date. The necessary co-ordination of the different factors of production can be obtained more easily in other ways: by choosing as Ministers for the separate Departments men of co-operative spirit and by setting up an effective War Cabinet on the 1916 model above them.

The same argument applies to other departmental groupings which have been suggested. In theory there is something to be said in favour of grouping under one Minister such offices as agriculture and food, or the three Defence Departments. But it is doubtful whether such grouping yields any advantages which cannot be obtained by the easier method of an effective War Cabinet ready to give decisions between the Departments as they stand. On the other hand, grouping has two grave disadvantages; first, that the super-Minister in charge of a group of Departments is almost bound to interfere with the sense of responsibility and speed of action of his subordinates; second, that he is almost bound to become absorbed in executive details, leaving him no time to think, to read, to discuss, to plan ahead. The tradition that a Minister of a named Department is responsible for everything done by that Department, and therefore must be prepared to know about everything, if asked, is strong and not easily shaken in this country.

The essence of the 1916 War Cabinet was that it consisted of Ministers without Portfolio, that is to say without Departments. This is what is wanted today. But Ministers without Portfolio need not be Ministers without specialization. Assuming a British War Cabinet of the present Prime Minister and four or at most five colleagues—the strongest practical minds in the country—one of these colleagues might well become chairman of a Defence Committee, bringing together the three Services; another might be chairman of an Imperial War Council (with the right of the whole Council to attend meetings of the Cabinet for imperial issues); two others might divide the various problems of industry and the home front; one of these, or yet another, might lead the House of Commons. But these would be their special, not their exclusive, spheres. And they would be Ministers without Ministries or Permanent Secretaries.

On the face of it, and as conceived by most of those who have asked for it, the appointment of a Minister of Production is irrelevant to the main issue of war government. But the considerations set out above against re-creating a Ministry of Munitions have clearly had their practical effect already in the detailed arrangements defining the scope of the new Minister. The executive responsibilities of all the other Departments now concerned with production, including the Ministry of Labour and National Service, are formally reserved. The new Minister of Production might conceivably move in the direction of becoming a War Cabinet Minister specialized in a particular field but without executive responsibilities or a Department of his own. He might conceivably become the first of a new set of War Cabinet Ministers without Portfolio. But he should be one only out of several of that type.

The origin of the Government in 1916–18 and the principles upon which it was founded have been described by no one better than by the Prime Minister of today. In his account of The World Crisis, describing the meeting between Mr. Lloyd George and Mr. Bonar Law which led to the new Government in December, 1916, Mr. Churchill states :—

> The main principle uniting the two Ministers was that the existing Cabinet system whereby the executive heads of the various Departments each with his special point of view formed the supreme directing authority was not adapted to the unprecedented peril of the time.*

The appointment of a Minister of Production, as now arranged without authority over labour, means that there is no method short of action by the Prime Minister himself to co-ordinate the vital factors in production. It adds, therefore, to the burdens of the Prime Minister, instead of lightening them. It does nothing to give to the Prime Minister colleagues who can be trusted to decide large issues of policy wisely because they have had time for thought and forethought. It cannot be the last step in reconstruction if the nation is to have leadership adequate to the unprecedented peril of 1942.

* The World Crisis, vol. iii, p. 249.

2

A NEW SPIRIT FOR TOTAL WAR*

THE recent changes in the Government are a long step forward towards more effective conduct of the war.† But they are a first step only, of little avail unless change of form in government leads to changes of spirit and of policy. Three such changes, at least, are required, for in three fields at least we have carried into this third year of fighting ways of thought and action which are desirable in peace but dangerous in war.

First, we have carried on into the war with too little change the peace-time economic structure of the country and the system of economic rewards. We have continued to rely upon individual capitalism with its accompanying machinery of wage-bargaining, even though the excess profits tax and other financial relations between the State and business managers have deprived both private capitalism and wage-bargaining of their logical basis. We have left vital production in the hands of individuals whose duty it was to consider not solely the needs of the nation in war but the interests of shareholders and of what would be the position of their businesses after the war. We have allowed some of the farmers' spokesmen to talk as if putting their utmost effort into the use of our land depended upon the terms of a price bargain. We have, generally against the advice of economists, treated our workpeople as if they were "economic men," unamenable even in war to any motive stronger than personal gain.

Meanwhile the State has set out to direct the employment of all men without taking responsibility for ensuring a fair distribution of income. The main evil of this economic

* *The Times*, 17th March, 1942. *News Chronicle*, 19th March, 1942.
† See Note 3.

policy is not the bogey of inflation nor is it that a few
people may make large profits or large wages: its evils lie,
partly in the indefensible and dangerous inequalities that
have resulted between civilians and the members of the
fighting forces, between different civilians, and between
different businesses; partly in the fact that bribery by price
or wage is often an ineffective spur to output.

The time calls for two changes: first, for the State to
take direct responsibility for the control of vital industries and for the distribution of income; second, for
assertion of the principle that service rather than personal
gain should be the mainspring of war effort in industry as
in fighting. To say that wage and price bargains are out
of place in war is not to criticize the actions or to deny the
value of associations of workpeople and of employers.
Trade unions are an essential element in the British
democracy, and for peace I, at least, want trade unions
after the British model—autonomous associations, pur-
suing sectional ends—rather than trade unions after the
Russian model—associations forming part of the regular
machinery of the State. But is it too much to suggest
that, in war and for the war only, our trade unions should
become, after the Russian model, the conscious agents of
national policy?

To say, again, that service rather than gain should be
the main motive for all men's acts in war is not to say that
exceptional effort should never receive special reward;
exceptional effort—to put it no higher—needs exceptional
sustenance and freedom from economic care. But to treat
private gain as the dominant motive for war effort is to
slander our people; British workpeople are not by nature
profiteers, and can be made to act as profiteers in war only
by mismanagement or misleading. If it is true that output
of our factories improved suddenly when Russia came
into the war, this does not mean that the workers are
stupid in preferring Russia to their own country; it means

that in war the most effective spur to heroic effort is an idea, not the hope of personal gain.

Second, we have carried on with too little change in our political as well as our economic structure. We need now to substitute national government for coalition government. The organization of parties is a necessary element in peacetime; a one-party State is not a democracy. Since party organizations will be needed after the war, they must be kept alive during the war, but war government should not be based on them. To base government in war on a coalition of party organizations is to appoint or retain Ministers not because they are the best men for their work but because of their political aptitudes and relations. To do this is to entrust the fortunes of the country to men of divided loyalty. Just because a party leader has responsibilities for his party after the war he cannot even in war be single-minded. To blame business men for conducting their businesses in war with an eye to post-war advantage, and at the same time leave the government of the country in the hands of men who should feel—and do feel—a duty to their parties, is to strain at gnats and swallow camels whole and kicking.

In the circumstances of today reliance on party coalition as the basis of war government has the added weakness that the House of Commons itself gets increasingly recruited, not by popular election, but by nomination of the party machines. It was a misfortune when the present Prime Minister accepted the leadership of a party and thus consecrated the practice of party bargaining as the basis of war government. In the recent change of Government, the misfortune might have been redeemed and a good change made even better, if the change could have come through the Prime Minister resigning at once his office and his party leadership, and being invited, as himself the one indispensable leader and saviour of the country two years ago, to form a fresh Government free of all party trammels.

This argument does not mean that a war Government should take no thought of post-war problems: on the contrary, it should set in hand preparation of plans whereby the evils of peace—poverty, squalor, preventible disease, inequality of opportunity, waste of abilities—may be abolished after it has abolished the evil of war. The war Government should think ahead for the nation, but not for itself; its members should look neither to their own futures nor to those of their friends. They should be chosen for themselves, nor for their parties; they should be a suicide club prepared to die politically that Britain and civilization may live.

Third, with our peace-time economic and political structure, we have carried on into war our national habits of compromise and procrastination. In one of his most brilliant and penetrating passages dealing with the last war, the present Prime Minister has described the different needs of peace and war in the arts of government: has emphasized the advantage in peace of proceeding slowly but surely by conciliation and compromise, of allowing time for change of opinion and melting away of objections:

> The object in time of Peace is often to keep the Nation undisturbed by violent passions and able to move forward in a steady progress through the free working of its native energies and virtues. Many an apparently insoluble problem solves itself or sinks to an altogether lower range if time, patience and phlegm are used. . . .
>
> In War everything is different. There is no place for compromise in War. . . . In War, the clouds never blow over, they gather unceasingly and fall in thunderbolts. . . . Clear leadership, violent action, rigid decisions one way or another form the only path not only of victory, but of safety and even of mercy.

The State cannot afford division or hesitation at its executive centre. To humour a distinguished man, to avoid a fierce dispute, nay, even to preserve the governing instrument itself, cannot, except as an alternative to sheer anarchy, be held to justify half-measures. The peace of the Council may for the moment be won, but the price is paid on the battle-field by brave men marching forward against unspeakable terrors in the belief that conviction and coherence have animated their orders.*

The fundamental difference is that in war the pace is set by the enemy, not by the conversion-time of whatever may be the slowest minds in Britain; leaders must take the risks of leading. Yet, in this country, since May 1940, as before, we have had a Government which in many ways has followed public opinion instead of leading it. We have had—not, indeed, from the Prime Minister, but from some of his lieutenants—delay, compromise, procrastination, both practised and defended.

Ten months ago, in urging a particular measure of compulsion† in spite of the shock that it might give to old ways of thought, I suggested as a guiding principle that, if there was any useful measure which we should be prepared in extremity to take rather than surrender, we should take that measure at once, without waiting for extremity. If there was any doubt that my principle was right in the state of the war ten months ago, there can be no doubt today. Compromise and procrastination, defended in the name of national unity, have helped to bring us within sight of defeat. While we haggle for agreement, in the enslaved lands each day hundreds or thousands of helpless men and women and children die and millions suffer, waiting for

---

* *The World Crisis*, vol. iii, p. 239. I have printed this passage at slightly greater length here than was possible in the restricted space of an article.

† Military conscription of women.

our rescue. If we cannot win a sense of urgency from our own danger, we should do so from the thought of the butcheries and barbarities which cover Europe.

War is not peace and peace is not war. The time has come—in truth it came long ago—to strip away the trappings and frivolities of peace; when we beat plough-shares into swords, we should exchange also three other P's for S's: profit for service, party for State, procrastination for speed. Some of the things said here may give offence, but anger against them will not shake their truth, and if they are true they must be said—for our country is in peril and civilization is at stake. The war has to be won outright, for compromise with evil is defeat. But that which we fight is as powerful as it is evil.

On a sober review of the forces on each side and of the immense industrial gains already made by our enemies, can we hope to win the war outright unless we wage it by land and sea and air, at home and abroad, in our factories and in our fields, with the fanaticism of a holy war, unless we make of it a crusade to rescue the liberties of mankind and millions of our fellows? A crusade cannot be conducted on a cash basis; it cannot be led to victory through timid counsels or by men of divided loyalty. Let us now wage total war not defensively for possessions but offensively against evil, not just to preserve our island home, but for the ideals of tolerance, fair play, freedom of thought and speech, kindliness, and the value of the individual soul, which from our home we have tried to spread throughout the world. Let us wage a war of all the people in the spirit of Cromwell's Army, of men "making not money but that which they took for the public felicity to be their end."

3

THE MEANING OF TOTAL WAR*

ONE of the common sayings of today is that this war is or should be a total war. What do we mean by total war? Some people when they use that phrase are thinking of the nation as a whole—they mean that the war has to be waged not only by fighting men but by workers keeping up production, in fields and factories and mines, and by housewives in their homes, keeping up the health and strength of their families. But to me total war means also something else; it means total for each individual—that each individual should be putting the whole—not just part of himself—into war effort.

Of course, that does not mean that every human being in the country should be doing now something so directly concerned with war that he would not be doing it in peace. The human beings of this country include, thank Heaven, the children, and there must be people looking after those children; there must be food and clothes and houses for everybody; there are countless necessary tasks common to war and to peace.

Of course, also, some of those who are now failing to put the whole of themselves into the war effort, are failing not through any fault of their own. They are longing to do war work but they do not get the chance at all or they get only half used when they would like to be fully used. The nation isn't yet fully organized for war—most of us have ideas about things which it seems to us that the Government might do better.

But tonight I'm not concerned with things which only the Government can put right. I'm speaking to ourselves as individual citizens, about ways in which we may fail to

* Radio Address, Sunday, 22nd March, 1942.

be total in war through causes within our control, about what we might do to put that right and why we ought to be total in war. Let me give some examples. In the factories engaged in making munitions the one thing that matters now is immediate output, both in quality and in quantity. If the manager in charge of a factory thinks of anything but that, if he thinks, for instance, of dividends for his shareholders now or later, or of what his factory may be used for after the war and how it can be made most useful or profitable in peace, then he is not total in the war—he's half out of the war, half neutral. If a workman in a factory or on a farm or in a mine does less or worse work than his best, if he is less regular in attendance than he could be, either because he thinks he is not getting paid enough or because he is getting paid so well that he does not want to earn more, or because he thinks that he ought not to pay Income Tax on earnings—that is not total war. It's being half out of the war—half neutral. In peace time it is right to make conditions about one's work. In peace it is reasonable to stop working when one thinks one has earned enough. For managers and for workmen alike that's an essential part of freedom: to be able to choose leisure, seeing more of one's family, time for study or just going to the races, in place of making more money. But many things right in peace are utterly wrong in war. Total war for the worker, as for the soldier, sailor or airman or the fire fighter, means going all out when called on, irrespective of reward. Moreover, being total in war is not simply a question of how one behaves at work; one can wage total war or fail to wage it in one's home, by being a saver or a waster, a cheerer or a grouser. If, for instance, a housewife whose man is away from her, in one of the Services or on war production, keeps on worrying him about her domestic troubles, nags at him to come home, without leave, or interrupting his work—she is not total in war.

I have given these examples not to suggest that they are common: it doesn't matter how common or rare they are. They oughtn't to happen at all. I believe that nearly all of us want to be total in this war: most who fail do so for reasons beyond their control; sometimes when the reason is within our control, it is not any petty or selfish reason. Many people in peace devote themselves to a cause—they serve a movement like trade unionism or co-operation, they work for a political party, they seek to remedy a social injustice. Some go on doing so in war, even though this may mean reducing the war effort, by disagreements or by occupying the time and thought of Ministers and managers on matters irrelevant to the war. That is failing to be total in war for an unselfish motive, but it is failure none the less.

There is another thing which sometimes holds an individual back from total war: that's our British sense of justice. We're ready to do or bear anything if we get fair play—but we're apt to ask for fair play first. That means sometimes that if we are asked to do something or to bear some hardship we hesitate, because we are not sure that the same demand is being made of all our fellows. That is right and reasonable in peace. But it is very dangerous in war. The Government ought to see that the hardships and burdens of war are distributed as fairly as possible. But it isn't at all easy to ensure fair play for everybody at any time, still less in war. And quite plainly in war we can't afford the time to insist on fair play *first* in every case. We've got to take what's given us, do to the utmost everything that comes to us to do, and trust to getting justice later. That alone is total war. That's how it was on Trafalgar Day. Nelson's signal was "England expects that every man this day will do his duty." Nelson's signal was *not* "England expects that every man this day will see that everyone else is doing his duty before he does his own."

Total war means living in and for the present—for war

and not for peace, without allowing thought of what may happen to one in peace to lessen one's effort in war. Does that sound grim and horrible? Perhaps it does. War is a grim and horrible business, and we do not make it any less so by shirking the fact. But that is only part of the answer to my question. There are three other things I want to say about it.

First, though war work is often grim and exhausting, that doesn't mean that one mayn't enjoy doing it. To go all out as one of a team is fine. To work with people with whom in peace one may have differed is one of the consolations of war.

Second, saying that the individual should be total in war without thought of his personal future, does not mean that the Government of the country should take no thought for the future. The Government even while waging war should be framing plans for peace, plans to abolish the evils from which we have suffered in peace, after we have ended this evil of war. Of course, our Government is doing just that and I happen to have been working for the Government on one side of that—the question of planning insurance against economic insecurity of every kind. I can't tell you of course just what the plans are likely to be, but I can say that I've no doubt at all that we know how to abolish want through economic insecurity, and that it's in our power to do so as soon as the war ends, on one condition—that we've won the war. On that condition I sincerely believe that we're within sight of a world for all, far safer, far freer than anything that we have known.

Third, whether we like it or not, we really have no choice—we must be total in war—every one of us—if we don't want to lengthen the war and perhaps lose it in the end. To risk losing the war because we are thinking of our individual rights either now or afterwards, is just plain silliness. None of us will have any rights worth thinking about if Germany wins. Countries which tried to be neutral in this war haven't had much luck. They've been overrun themselves and been a danger to their neighbours. Individuals who weaken our war effort by standing out of total war are like those neutrals—doing no good for themselves and being a danger to the rest.

We must all wage total war for our own sakes, but having said that I want to say even more strongly, that we ought not to be fighting only for ourselves. We didn't begin the war that way. We ought not to be content merely to defend our own island now. Everybody will fight to defend his home; there's no merit in that. We, in Britain, ought to do better. The Russians are fighting magnificently because they're defending their homes, but I do not believe they'd be fighting so well for that alone. They are fighting also for ideas, for their ideals of how society should be organized. We, too, on this island have stood and stand for ideas—of tolerance, fair-play, freedom of speech and thought, kindliness, the value of the individual soul. Our fathers went out and spread those ideas all over the world; it is up to us to fight to keep them alive not only in this island, but in the world.

If you saw a bully kicking a child, you would not, before doing anything to stop him, wait to argue as to whose fault it was that the bully got loose: you would not ask whether the child was British; you would not look round and see whether it was not someone else's job to come to the rescue. You'd go straight in. That picture of the bully kicking the child is not fancy. It's a fact; it's what you would see with your own eyes if you could go freely about Europe. All over Europe you would see every day helpless men and women and children being killed by starvation or the bullet or bayonet. You'd see the same thing happening to our own people and the Chinese in Asia. Your way and mine of going in and putting the bully in the place where he belongs is for every man and woman of us at once to be as total in war as we can, and to do all we can to let the Government know that a total war is what we want, so that they needn't be afraid to take any measures of organization that are needed.

There was once in history a kind of war called the Crusades. Some of the Crusades at the end came to be waged for bad as well as for good motives—but they began as wars for no gain of power or wealth, as wars of the common people for an idea and a faith. That is the kind of war which we must wage today, a war of faith of all the people, to rescue the threatened freedom of mankind. That kind of war is needed, that's what the world expects of a people with our strength and our history, of the sons and daughters of the race which built the free British Commonwealth and founded the free United States of America. A war of faith is what the world is waiting for. Don't let it wait another moment.

THE NEW METER

THE NEW METER, MUM

Reproduced by permission of the Proprietors of the "Evening Standard"
(See Note 4)

4

THE FIVE CHRISTIAN STANDARDS*

In a letter appearing in *The Times* on 21st December, 1940, four leaders of the Churches in Britain accepted "five peace points" set out by Pope Pius XII, and laid down five propositions of their own, as standards by which economic situations and proposals may be tested. I have been asked as a guest speaker at this Conference to open the discussion of these standards. I will do so by commenting briefly on each of them in turn.

1. *Extreme inequality in wealth and possessions should be abolished.*

It is easy to agree with this proposition—on the ground that the object of acquiring wealth is human happiness, and that broadly speaking the same amount of wealth will yield more happiness, if it is distributed widely than if it is divided with great inequality. A pound buys the same amount of the same articles whoever spends it, but not the same amount of happiness. A pound to a poor man means more than a pound to a rich man—meets more urgent needs and therefore produces more happiness.

Most economists would agree with that. A few question it, on the ground that we can't compare one man with another; that the satisfaction which a rich and cultivated man gets out of foreign travel or rare books or pictures may be more important than the satisfaction of physical want of another man. That's a highly academic argument. The poor man's last shilling normally meets needs which the millionaire, like everyone else, would regard as more

* Address to Rochester Diocesan Conference, Caxton Hall, 10th November, 1942.

important than the needs on which the millionaire spends his last shilling. A step to greater equality of wealth is a step in the right direction, of using material resources for human happiness.

This general assent to the first of the five propositions is subject to three comments:

(a) The poor man doesn't in fact always spend his last shilling on more important satisfactions than the rich man. He may waste it—and so may the moderately rich man waste some of his money, while Mr. Rockefeller endows research to combat disease and to spread healing.

(b) The needs of the future are as vital as those of the present, but are not always felt as urgently. To eat the seed-corn for next year means starving next year. Savings are the seed-corn of industrial production. A rising standard of life depends on increasing use of instruments of production. The Soviet Union, in the early days of its industrial revolution, made its people go short of consumption goods, so that they might have factories and machines. Savings hitherto and investment have come out of superfluity of the rich. Wider distribution of wealth will require a correspondingly wider distribution of the obligations and functions of wealth, including the obligation of saving for investment in capital goods.

(c) The proposition involves abolishing extreme inequality only, not all inequality. That is right in practice and in principle. In Britain there is marked inequality even of working class incomes. No country has in fact attempted equality—certainly not the Soviet Union. Economic rewards for effort and economic punishment for failure of effort are the alternative to the chain-gang. What some people call wage-slavery is the alternative to real slavery and is the condition of freedom. We can see that by considering one of the differences between the full freedom which we should have in peace and the limited freedom with which we ought to be content in war. It is to my mind one of the essential freedoms of peace that one should be at liberty to stop work when one has earned as much as one wants, should have the choice between earning and leisure. But that's not permissible in war. If the work that any man is doing—as a soldier, miner or engineer, or in any other occupation—is necessary to the war effort, he oughtn't to feel at liberty to play when he wants, because he has already earned all the money he wants. He must be content in war to forego one of the essential liberties of peace.

To press for absolute equality of incomes for all men is unpractical. It is also a wrong aim, for it means attaching excessive importance to material things and treating envy as a master passion of mankind.

These three comments do not weaken my whole-hearted assent to this first standard for testing our economic institutions. Extreme inequalities of income are evil. At one end of the scale extreme inequality takes the form of want of the physical means of subsistence. At the other end of the scale· it gives excessive power divorced from responsibility.

2. *Every child, regardless of race or class, should have equal opportunities of education, suitable for the development of his peculiar capacities.*

This proposition at first sight commands easy and general assent, for two reasons: the fullest possible use of capacities of each individual is necessary both for his own happiness, since happiness lies in activity, and for the prosperity and progress of the society of which he is a member.

But a second view suggests that there are some words in this proposition that need to be examined further: the words "equal" and "regardless of race or class." What determines the race or class of a child? His parenthood, that is, his family. If we re-write the second proposition, "Every child, regardless of his family, should have equal opportunities for education," we see that it must be considered in the light of the third proposition: "the family as a social unit must be safeguarded." Let us look at the two propositions together.

3. *The Family as a social unit must be safeguarded.*

Are the second and third propositions consistent with one another? The family as a social unit is an institution for favouring particular children, not on account of their capacities but because of their parentage, that is, their race or class. It is an institution aiming at inequality of opportunity. That is why logical thorough-going communists like Plato and socialists like Bernard Shaw have disliked the family. Ought the family to be allowed to stand for inequality of opportunity? Yes, for two reasons:

(*a*) Family life, its responsibilities and its cares, are the material of which most of human happiness for most people is made. Charles Darwin summed up happiness as: "Work and the domestic affections." The work which different men find to do is of differing degrees of importance and interest. For a few it is an absorbing vocation, a complete life in itself; for many it must be dull and heavy. But the domestic affections are for all men and women. The family is the means of vicarious immortality through children, the stepping-stone from selfishness to service, the common heritage and bond of all mankind.

Through it each of us can project himself into the future. Through it, in trying to do better for the next generation than we have done for ourselves, we get our second chance.

(b) Heredity is a basic fact. The children of different parents are different in capacity. Heredity is not invariable; children of exceptional capacity may be born in almost any family; children of little capacity may be born of highly capable parents. But that, taking large numbers, the children of the more capable parents will, on the average, be more capable themselves, is undeniable. In leaving it possible for parents who by special service to the community acquire special rewards to favour their children because they are their children, one works with nature—not against her.

It may be objected that special service by the parents does not lead to special rewards—that wealth in Britain today is not distributed by service to the community: that great wealth and all the power that it brings may be acquired now, not by service, but by chance or exploitation of a strategic position: that the best servants of the community have often less reward than the selfish or useless. That is true in part at least. The remedy lies not in destroying the family but in amending the system of economic rewards. If incomes were adjusted to services completely, those who earned larger incomes ought to be allowed to use them for their children.

This emphasis on the importance of the family isn't a doctrine of aristocratic exclusiveness. The family is the most general of all human institutions. The passion to do the best one can for one's own children is nearly universal.

Nor does the preservation of the family as a social unit imply either acceptance of the present distribution of economic rewards as in accord with justice or a belief that enough has already been done to give opportunity according to capacity, regardless of race or class, i.e. regardless of family.

Nothing like enough has yet been done. The human family will continue to favour its own children. The State, as the general parent of all the children in the community, must enter where the family fails, and in giving opportunity should do so regardless of race or class. The State should see that every child gets all the opportunities that it deserves. Our fathers and mothers will go on trying to secure for each of us a little more than we deserve. If we all had exactly our deserts who would escape whipping?

4. *The sense of a Divine Vocation must be restored to a man's daily work.*

I shall say relatively little of this—not because it is unimportant—but for a purely personal reason. It so happens that I was not brought up in any religious faith and have never been a member of any religious community.

But I find no difficulty in attaching a meaning to this principle, which to me is important and which to you, I hope, will not seem wrong. It means to me that there should be something in the daily life of every man and woman which he or she does for no personal reward or gain, does ever more and more consciously as a mark of the brotherhood and sisterhood of all mankind.

To take that as one's ideal is not idle dreaming. Serving, exhausting oneself without thought of personal reward— isn't that what most women do most of their lives in peace or war? Isn't it what nearly all men are ready to do in war? Isn't it the mark of all those who in the judgment of their fellows are truly great, in peace or in war?

The manager of some of our largest war factories told me the other day that the way in which the women in his factories were working was marvellous; they were doing even better than the men. I asked him whether he thought

this might be because most women had the habit of working not for pay, but for service, in their homes: they never
related the amount of their effort to what they were going
to get by it for themselves. He said that very likely that was
the explanation. I wish we had made greater use of the
appeal for service, and less use of the appeal to the pocket
in the conduct of this war on the home front.

For me, then, to have the sense of Divine Vocation means
that in the daily life of each of us there should be something done, not by instinct, but more and more consciously,
without thought of reward, whether it is part of our paid
work or not. There should be something that is spending
ourselves, not getting anything. There should be something that in marking the brotherhood and sisterhood of
man, leads to the fatherhood of God.

5. *The resources of the earth should be used as God's gifts to
the whole human race and used with due consideration for
the needs of the present and future generations.*

This can be accepted, with due regard to two practical
considerations. One is that the resources of the earth are
not spread evenly throughout the world. Some parts of
the earth are definitely richer in resources—beneath the
surface or in the climate—than other parts. The other is
that it is inevitable that particular portions of the earth
should become occupied by particular human groups—
united in speech or character.

The world cannot be governed as one, without barriers
of national boundaries.

But the proposition gets support from economics.
Division of labour, specialization and exchange increase
wealth. Whether the natural resources of a nation are great
or small, they can be made more fruitful by co-operation
with other nations, than by isolation. Freer trade makes
for wealth, and beggar-my-neighbour economic policies
mean in the end beggar-myself. Use of the resources of the

earth as God's gifts to the whole human race and not to sections of the race makes for the prosperity of all.

Conclusion

The conclusion of this brief review is that all the five propositions laid down by the leaders of the Churches, as standards for the testing of our economic institutions deserve our support. If I have to choose between them, I put the third proposition before the second, though there is no necessary conflict. The first is the most certain and the most practical. The fourth and fifth are perhaps the most important, underlying all the rest. Only as men come to see themselves as part of a larger whole, as children of one Father, can the selfishness and the strife which lead to self-destruction be banished from the world.

5

MAINTENANCE OF EMPLOYMENT*

AT the present stage of this savage and critical war, how much time and thought ought we to spend in discussing what may happen after the war, in planning for reconstruction? Obviously, not many of us ought to spend much of our time upon that subject. The war, if we are going to get through it with success, must be total war: it is taxing and is going still more to tax all our strength. One of the faults which I, with others, find in the design of our central Government is that somehow it has not brought home to everybody sufficiently the urgency of total war and the difference between what is suitable for war and what is suitable for peace. It has not done so, I think, because in the central Government of the country, as we have had it since the beginning of this war and up to this moment, we have kept too much of peace-time methods, of the old forms of Cabinet and Ministerial responsibility, of party politics.

That is a question on which I've said a good deal in the past.† With a different form of central Government, I believe that we should now be further on towards winning the war. Today I'm concerned with a different question. Is it a help or a hindrance to winning the war to concern ourselves with what is to happen after the war is won? My answer to this question is that it is a help.

There are three ways of winning a war: by relying on speed and efficiency to deal a knock-out blow, by the mistakes of the enemy, by one's own staying power. Whatever we may hope from the first two ways we cannot afford in this war to neglect the third way. There is no

---

* Address to Engineering Industries Association 30th July, 1942.
† See Papers 1 and 2.

reason to doubt the natural staying power of our people, but there is every reason to strengthen that staying power. The Government can strengthen staying power by convincing the people that it is taking reconstruction seriously.

Whatever the nature of other peoples, I am certain that it is correct of any nation, like our own, in which freedom is not a surface veneer, but an inveterate habit, that we will refuse even in the worst of wars to give up thinking about peace; we are waging war not for its own sake, not for dominion, but for peace. Our staying power will be increased, in proportion as we can be given confidence that the peace which will come at the end of this war will be better than peace as we have known it before. That is why thinking about reconstruction is one of the ways of ensuring victory, and something worth doing even today. That is why you, who are all busy people, engaged on vital war production, have come to discuss with me some of the problems of reconstruction.

THE FIVE GIANTS

Reconstruction has many sides, international and domestic. On the domestic side one can define its aims best by naming five giant evils to be destroyed—Want, Disease, Ignorance, Squalor and Idleness. Today I am going to say little or nothing about any of the first four giants. Destruction of Want means ensuring that every citizen, in return for service, has income sufficient for his subsistence and that of his dependents both when he is working and when he cannot work. Want is really the subject of the enquiry which I have been making as Chairman of the Inter-Departmental Committee on Social Insurance and the Allied Services. That is, in effect, an enquiry as to how far we can go by development of social insurance and other services to ensure that no one in this country lacks the actual means of subsistence, even when unemployed or sick, or injured or old, or having lost a breadwinner.

The second giant—Disease—is one against which I am glad to think there is now a general move and a growing and, I hope, an effective demand for putting the health service of the country—preventive, curative, palliative—upon an altogether better and larger basis.

The attack on Ignorance is a matter of education. It means having more scholars and better schools. But it is not just a question of raising the school age: it is a question of the kind of education that we give at school, and it is even more a question of adult education.

By the giant Squalor I mean all those evils which come through the unplanned, disorderly growth of cities, bearing in its train congestion, bad housing, waste of energy of wage-earners in travelling and of housewives in struggling with needless dirt and difficulties at home, needless destruction of natural and historic beauty. Attack on Squalor means better location of industry and population and a revolution in housing.

Each of these four giants—Want, Disease, Ignorance, Squalor—would be a more than ample subject for discussion today and over many days. This afternoon I shall speak only of the fifth giant—Idleness. Can we hope to destroy Idleness after the war and, if so, by what methods? Destruction of Idleness means ensuring for every citizen a reasonable opportunity of productive service and of earning according to his service. It means maintenance of employment of labour and our other resources. Idleness is the largest and fiercest of the five giants and the most important to attack. If the giant Idleness can be destroyed, all the other aims of reconstruction come within reach. If not, they are out of reach in any serious sense and their formal achievement is futile. To hold out hopes, to announce a determination that at all costs we will prevent mass unemployment, is the most important of all reconstruction aims. The people of Britain today do not look back to the time before the war, as in the last war the people of Britain looked back upon the time before that war, as something to which they wish to return. This difference of attitude has its source in memories of the mass unemployment which ruined so many lives between the two wars from 1920 to 1939. In regard to that, British people today have only one sentiment: "Never again."

What are the conditions of successful attack upon the giant Idleness, of preventing mass unemployment in the aftermath of the present war?

War Solution of Unemployment

One way of trying to answer that question is to look at the conditions under which unemployment is reduced to insignificance today. Unemployment has been practically abolished twice in the lives of most of us—in the last war and in this war. Why does war solve the problem of unemployment which is so insoluble in peace? The main conditions of the war solution of unemployment are twofold:

(i) The Government on behalf of the nation prepares a schedule of vital needs to be met (men to fight, arms, ships, food, raw materials), makes a plan for the use of all productive resources to meet those needs, and secures that use either directly by regulations and instructions or indirectly by control of purchasing power.

(ii) The Government has one need for men without effective limit of numbers and with no restrictions in the choice of men to meet it. No one physically fit to be a sailor, soldier or airman can refuse to be one if called on or be prevented from becoming one by the opposition of those who are sailors, soldiers or airmen already. There are no craft barriers in regard to the Armed Forces: no right of an individual to refuse to enter them on the ground that he belongs to a different trade: nothing to keep out those who wish to enter if they will be useful there. Moreover, in civilian industry, craft barriers, though not wholly abolished, as in the Armed Forces, are greatly reduced.

The two conditions on which in war-time unemployment gets abolished are comprehensive planning by the State of the use of all important resources and the making of those resources, including labour, completely fluid. Can we hope to accomplish the same full use of resources in the aftermath of war, except on something like the same conditions?

Maintenance of productive employment means adjustment of productive resources to real needs. In time of peace, in all countries other than Russia, this adjustment has been carried out in the main by price mechanism. In so far as the price mechanism has failed to do what was desired, most States have limited themselves to seeking remedies of a general financial nature, that is to say, they have still worked through the price mechanism, endeavouring to manipulate the volume of purchasing power in general, but not to direct it down particular channels. In times of total war adjustment of resources to needs is carried out by complete State planning. Shall the aftermath of this war be treated by the former methods of peace or by the methods of war? On the face of it, the experience of 1920–1939 suggests that the former methods of peace are unlikely to accomplish the object in view with even tolerable success, and that there are probably two unavoidable conditions for the maintenance of productive employment after the present war, namely (*a*) continuance of fluidity of labour and resources, and (*b*) continuance of national planning.

FLUIDITY OF LABOUR AND NATIONAL PLANNING

What do I mean by fluidity of labour? I mean, on the one hand, absence of barriers against entry of labour into the trades in which it is wanted, and absence of resistance by labour to moving to new trades. We need fluidity of labour in war because passage from peace to war changes all our needs and calls for a corresponding change in the use of our resources; that means a change of the occupations of our people. We need fluidity of labour in the aftermath of war, for exactly the same reason. Our needs change again as peace succeeds war; they do not change back again to exactly the same needs as those of the peace before.

Re-adjustment to peace-time needs of resources distorted by war will involve great changes of present occupations: it cannot be carried out if sectional barriers obstruct the entry of fresh labour into growing trades or if the right of individuals to remain idle on benefit rather than to do work that is offered to them on fair terms is recognized. Nothing that any British Government could have done between the two wars would have made it possible to find work for all the coal-miners of Britain as coal-miners, for the shipbuilders as shipbuilders, for textile operatives as textile operatives. When the tides of the last war receded they left a changed world, with less demand for our exports, and therefore with less demand for the services of such men. If such men were to be used, some of them had to change their jobs. Fluidity of labour and other resources means that men are willing to work and free to work, on proper terms, at what wants doing, even if it is something different from what they have been used to do before. To some extent the two conditions of national planning and fluidity of labour depend on one another. The way to remove restrictions on the movement of labour to trades where it is needed is to remove the fear of unemployment.

What do I mean by national planning? I mean that someone on behalf of the State must make a design of how the needs of its citizens can be met by use of their skill and labour applied to their material resources. There's no question that we shall have needs enough and more than enough to use all our resources. It is easy to think of innumerable things that will be needed in this country—houses and their labour-saving equipment, schools, hospitals, transport, all the replacement of everything that we have missed in the war. But we mustn't think only of things to make for use at home. We are going to end this war poorer than when we entered it, by having lost our foreign investments, the savings our fathers made and which enabled us to get many imports from abroad without paying for them. We shall have lost a great deal of our position as ship-owners, as common carriers in international trade. To feed ourselves and to obtain raw materials which can only come from abroad we shall have to make goods for export and find markets for these goods. Houses, schools, hospitals are all excellent things—there's little chance of our ever having too many of them. But from the point of view of economic policy after the war, houses, schools and hospitals all suffer from a common disadvantage. We can neither eat them or export them, to pay for the food and the raw materials that we need from abroad. We've got to think of things to export also. They must be part of the plan.

National planning means that someone on behalf of the State shall prepare a schedule of the things that are required including purchasing power abroad, and, on the other side, a schedule of the resources that are available—a reckoning of the number and kinds of factories and of the number and kinds of men and women available for production. In the aftermath of war resources and needs must be brought into relation to one another by deliberate State action. We cannot trust the price mechanism. Passage from peace to war and passage from war to peace are each alike times of rapid change in the direction of our productive effort. For rapid change direct action by the State, not indirect action through the price mechanism, is essential.

But national planning by the State does not mean that everything must be done by the State. Far from it. There is a difference between making a design and executing it. Exactly what the execution of a national plan would mean in practice, how much would be done by the State, how much and under what controls would be done by associations and individuals, cannot be stated till the plan has been prepared. But it is possible to name some things which national planning would not mean—to begin by defining it negatively.

National planning does not mean that the whole plan, when made, is carried out directly by the State. It may, and probably does, mean replacement of competitive private enterprise for profit by public monopoly enterprise not for profit in certain fields; but private and public enterprise alike will work within limits set by a general design.

National planning does not mean administration of everything from Whitehall: one essential of a good plan is devolution, regional and industrial.

National planning does not mean that we can do without leadership, management, initiative in industry, any more than it means that we can do without discipline.

ESSENTIAL LIBERTIES

National planning does not mean surrender of any essential citizen liberties; whatever may suit other countries, a plan for Britain must preserve freedom of opinion and its expression, in public or private, in speech or writing; freedom of association for political and other purposes; freedom of movement and choice of useful occupations; personal property and an income of one's own, with freedom to save or spend it. These are essential liberties. They must be preserved. They can be preserved.

What about private enterprise—the right to manage one's own business? Private enterprise at private risk is a good ship and a ship that has brought us far on the journey to higher standards of living and of leisure. No one with any regard to facts will deny the merits of this system or part from it lightly. But private enterprise at private risk is a ship for fair weather and open seas. For the ice-bound straits of war we find in practice that we need a vessel of a different build, sturdier if less speedy, a *Fram* like Nansen's not a China clipper. To find our way out of war into peace again we may need such a sturdier vessel still.

In any case, private control of means of production, with the right to employ others at a wage in using those means, whatever may be said for it or against it on other grounds, cannot be described as an essential liberty of the British people. Not more than a tiny fraction of British people have ever enjoyed that right. I myself have never owned any means of production except a fountain pen and an occasional garden tool.

The question of how to carry out a national plan after the war is a question not of essential liberties but of machinery: it is a question to which at the moment I do not feel that I know the answer.

DESIGN IN ALTERNATIVES

I do not see how one should be expected to know the answer until one has made a design. It would, I believe, be possible to make the design for the conduct of our economic affairs after the war in alternatives: one, preserving a great deal of private ownership and private enterprise; one, preserving very little and nationalizing most important industries; one, perhaps taking a half-way line between these two designs. The essential thing, however, is to make the design. Only by thinking about it can we reach a conclusion as to what is needed after the war to maintain employment.

On these two conditions—of national planning and fluidity of labour—is maintenance of employment possible after the war? I believe that it is. Why should it not be possible? The needs of peace are as unlimited as the needs of war; if they can be scheduled and brought into relation to resources, we can use our resources fully in meeting our needs fully. That is just a problem of organization. There will be great difficulties of transition from war to peace and to suit the changed economic conditions of the world that will result from the war. There will be difficulties of transition, but why should we believe that they are insuperable? Development of our export trade is essential in order to obtain the food and raw materials which hitherto have come to us as payment for overseas investment. But the people who grow this food and raw materials will want to send us what they have grown or made and will be willing to let us pay for it. International trade can only be developed after the war in agreement with the other countries, but must we assume that such agreements will be difficult or impossible?

Maintenance of employment will be possible in a world of peaceful intentions, but it will be possible only at a price. Nothing worth having can be had for nothing; every good thing has its price. Maintenance of employment—prevention of mass idleness after the war—is a good thing worth any price, except war or surrender of essential liberties. It can be had without that surrender, but not without giving up something; chiefly, we must give up our darling vice of not looking ahead as a nation.

For the individual this war should be total; we'll not

get through, if individuals do less than their utmost for the war because they are thinking about their personal futures. But in order that individuals may be total in war, they must feel certain that the Government means business about reconstruction after the war.

NEED FOR A DECLARATION OF POLICY

We want our Government now to declare and to make us believe :—

(a) That, subject to leaving untouched the essential British liberties, it will be prepared to use the powers of the State to whatever extent may prove to be necessary, in order to maintain employment after the war;

(b) That it has set up an Economic General Staff (a body that doesn't exist today) to prepare a plan or plans for that purpose and to show just what will need to be done.

That must be said by our Government and believed. I do not know what chance there is of such a declaration or what sort of Government could make it and be believed. I am sure only that that is what we would like to see. The people of this country aren't looking for easy good times for all. Maintenance of employment doesn't mean easy times for all. It means opportunity for all: it is the chance for all of productive work and release of energy from paralysing fear.

We want our Government now to declare and to make us believe that it will be prepared to use the powers of the State to whatever extent may prove to be necessary, subject only to the preservation of essential citizen liberties, in order to maintain employment after the war. When that has been said, and believed, we shall be, as we are not now, past the corner which hides victory from our eyes.

We shall have, if not a second front in Europe, what is at least as important in winning the war—a second wind. We shall by that belief and purpose have energies beyond estimate released for war. We shall be united in combined attack on tyranny and savagery abroad and on Want, Disease, Ignorance, Squalor and Idleness at home. Let us become united now for total war and for a peace different from the last peace abroad and at home.

LOOK WHAT'S GOING IN!

Reproduced by permission of the Proprietors of the "Evening Standard"
(See Note 5)

6

PLAN FOR SOCIAL SECURITY*

THE Atlantic Charter, among other aims, speaks of securing for all "improved labour standards, economic advancement and social security." The Security Plan in my Report is a plan for turning the last two words "social security" from words into deeds, for securing that no one in Britain willing to work, while he can, is without income sufficient to meet at all times the essential needs of himself and of his family. That plan hasn't yet been considered by Government or Parliament. What I am speaking about tonight is simply the proposals which I have made.

The Security Plan has three sides to it. It includes first a scheme of all-in social insurance for cash benefits. It includes, second, a general scheme of children's allowances both when the responsible parent is earning and when he is not earning. It includes, third, an all-in scheme of medical treatment of every kind for everybody.

I shall not attempt here and now to explain the whole Plan to you. I hope that many of you will be able to get hold of the Report itself. You'll find it rather a long document. But for general purposes all that you need to read is Part I at the beginning and Part VI at the end; both these Parts are quite short and deal with matters of general interest to everybody. You needn't go to the other parts except to look up particular points in which you are interested.

The main feature of the Security Plan is an all-in scheme of social insurance. That scheme applies to all citizens and not only to those who work for employers. It doesn't apply in exactly the same way to all citizens; one can't very well insure a person who hasn't an employer—say a shop-

* Radio Address, 2nd December, 1942 (see Note 6).

keeper or a farmer—against unemployment, or insure a
person who doesn't work for gain at all against losing
his earnings through sickness. But for the things which
everyone needs—pensions in old age, funeral expenses,
medical treatment—everyone will be insured. And everyone will be insured for these and all the other benefits
appropriate to him and his family, by a single weekly
contribution paid through one insurance stamp.

With one exception, the social insurance scheme provides a flat rate of benefit irrespective of the amount of
the earnings that have been lost, for a flat contribution.
The benefit will be the same for unemployment and disability of all kinds and, after a transition period, for pensions on retirement; it is designed to be high enough by
itself to provide subsistence and prevent want in all normal
cases; and it will last as long as the unemployment or
disability lasts without a means test. The one exception
to the flat rate principle is that, if disability has resulted
from an industrial accident or disease, after thirteen weeks
disability benefit will be replaced by an industrial pension
proportionate to the earnings lost but not less than disability benefit.

In addition to unemployment and disability, the scheme
provides benefits to meet many other needs, including
maternity, widowhood and guardianship of children,
funeral expenses, training for new occupation.

In regard to old age, the scheme proposes a number of
changes. First it makes pensions universal, applying not
only to those who work for employers, as at present, but
to independent workers and to those who do not work
for gain at all. Second it makes pensions conditional on
retirement from work. Third, it makes those retirement
pensions adequate for subsistence—equal to unemployment and disability benefit—but brings them up to that
level only gradually during a transition period of twenty
years; during that period those who need more than they

can get as contributory pensions will have their needs met by adequate assistance pensions. Fourth, the scheme enables people who go on working after reaching the minimum retiring age of 65 for men or 60 for women to qualify for pensions above the basic level which they would get if they retired as soon as they reached that age. The object of the scheme isn't to force early retirement, but to leave men free to retire when they want to and encourage them to go on working while they can.

In introducing adequate pensions as of right, over a transition period, during which the rate of contributory pensions will rise gradually, the Plan in my Report for Britain follows the precedent of New Zealand. The Plan for Britain is based on the contributory principle of giving not free allowances to all from the State, but giving benefits as of right in virtue of contributions made by the insured persons themselves as well as by their employers and the State. For pensions, contributions naturally must be paid over a substantial transition period before pension age is reached.

Of course, one of the points in which everyone is interested is knowing what will be rates of benefit and of contribution. It isn't possible to be quite definite about that because the benefits are meant to cover the cost of all essentials, and we cannot tell for certain now what food, fuel, clothing and house-room are going to cost after the war. But assuming that the cost of living after the war is a little less than it is now, the provisional rate of benefit that I suggest in my Report is £2 a week for man and wife in unemployment, disability and as retirement pension. For a single person or for a man whose wife is also working the rate will be lower. Where prolonged disability has resulted from an industrial accident there will be an industrial pension of two-thirds of the earnings, but not less than would have been received for ordinary sickness; usually it will be a good deal more. To all these benefits, children's allowance at the rate of 8/– a week for each child will be added. These allowances will be paid for every child when the responsible parent is on benefit or pension and to every child but one when the responsible parent is earning. Taking children's allowances into account, a married man with two children will get 56/– a week without means test so long as unemployment or disability lasts. If he has been incapacitated by industrial accident or disease, he will get an industrial pension between 56/– and 76/– a week according to his earnings. A widow with two children to look after will get 40/– a week; a married woman who also works for gain will be able to get maternity benefit of 36/– a week for 13 weeks at the time of a birth of a child in order that she may give up work for that time. This will be in addition to a maternity grant of £4 available to all mothers.

To secure these and all the other benefits of the Plan the contribution required for an adult man in employment will be 4/3 a week from himself and 3/3 from his employer, with lower rates for women and for young persons. By making these contributions insured persons in employment will pay about one-quarter of the total value of the cash benefits received by them, exclusive of children's allowances and national assistance which will be there to cover the few cases which fall through the meshes of the insurance scheme. The other three-quarters of the cash benefits will come from employers and from the State. Children's allowances and national assistance will come wholly from the State.

The contributions named above include a payment for full medical service of every kind for the insured person and for all his dependents, at home and in hospital; general, specialist and consultant; nursing services; dental and ophthalmic treatment, all that is needed for restoration to health and prevention of disease. Exactly how this medical service should be organized, how doctors should be paid and how hospitals should be financed and controlled are matters left open in the Report for further enquiry. But in one way or other comprehensive medical treatment and rehabilitation are part of the whole plan. The national minimum for every citizen today should include being well, being as well as science applied to prevention and cure of disease can make him.

Of course the Security Plan means a lot of money. It means a Security Budget for social insurance, children's allowances, medical treatment and national assistance amounting to nearly £700 millions in 1945 and more than £850 millions twenty years later. Those are large figures compared with former Treasury budgets. But they are not large in relation to the total national income and the Security Plan is only a means of redistributing national income, so as to put first things first, so as to ensure abolition of want before the enjoyment of comforts. Most of this money is being spent already in other ways. The total addition to be found from taxes and rates as compared with the cost of· the present schemes is at most £86 millions in the first year of the scheme. I can't believe that that won't be within our means when the war ends.

The Plan, as I have set it out briefly, is a completion of what was begun a little more than thirty years ago when Mr. Lloyd George introduced National Health Insurance, and Mr. Winston Churchill, then President of the Board of Trade, introduced Unemployment Insurance. The man who led us to victory in the last war was the Minister responsible for Health Insurance. The Minister who more than thirty years ago had the courage and imagination to father the scheme of Unemployment Insurance, a thing then unknown outside Britain, is the man who is leading us to victory in this war; I'd like to see him complete as well the work that he began in social insurance then.

But this is only my personal hope. What I have been telling you about is simply my proposals to the Government. The Government are not committed in any way to anything that I have said. They've only just seen my Report, and you won't expect them to make up their minds —they oughtn't to make up their minds—without full consideration. But I hope that the Government and Parliament and you will like the Security Plan, when you have all had time to consider it, and will adopt it. Having begun to work on this problem of social security myself more than thirty years ago, having lived with it for the past eighteen months and discussed it with all the people who know most about it, I believe that this plan or something like it is what we need. It's the first step, though it is one step only, to turning the Atlantic Charter from words into deeds.

7

THIRD TIME LUCKY?*

SUMMARY OF REPORT BY SIR WILLIAM BEVERIDGE ON SOCIAL INSURANCE AND ALLIED SERVICES

THE Report makes a survey of the existing national schemes of social insurance and allied services and recommends a Plan for Social Security designed to abolish physical want, by ensuring for all citizens at all times a subsistence income and the means of meeting exceptional expenditure at birth, marriage and death. The schemes and services surveyed include health insurance, unemployment insurance, old age pensions, widows' and orphans' pensions, workmen's compensation for industrial accident and disease, non-contributory pensions for old age, public assistance and blind assistance. The Inter-departmental Committee of which Sir William Beveridge was Chairman and which made this survey received representations from 127 different organizations other than Government departments, and met on 48 occasions. The Report is made by Sir William Beveridge alone in view of the fact that the other members of the Committee were all civil servants, and the existence of the Committee does not mean that the Government is associated in any way whatever with the proposals of the Report, for which the Chairman alone is responsible.

The survey shows that in a system of social security better on the whole than can be found in almost any other country there are serious deficiencies which call for remedy and anomalies and lack of co-ordination which cause needless expenditure. The recommendations of the Report are based on a diagnosis of want, that is to say of

* 17th November, 1942 (see Note 7).

the circumstances in which, in the years just preceding
the present war, families and individuals in Britain
might lack the means of healthy subsistence. Social surveys
in a number of principal towns in Britain showed that want
was due either to interruption or loss of earning power
or to large families. The Plan for Social Security is a plan
for dealing with these two causes of want, by a double
redistribution of income—between times of earning and
not earning (by social insurance) and between times of
large and small family responsibilities (by children's
allowances). Social security for the purpose of the Report
is defined as maintenance of subsistence income. The main
feature of the Plan is a scheme of social insurance embody-
ing six fundamental principles: flat rate of subsistence
benefit; flat rate of contribution; unification of administrative responsibility; adequacy of benefit; comprehensiveness and classification (paras. 303–9).

The Plan is summarized in paragraph 19 of the Report
as follows:

    (i) The Plan covers all citizens without upper income
        limit, but has regard to their different ways of
        life; it is a plan all-embracing in scope of persons
        and of needs, but is classified in application.

    (ii) In relation to social security the population falls
        into four main classes of working age and two
        others below and above working age respectively,
        as follows:—

        I. Employees, that is persons whose normal
           occupation is employment under contract of
           service.

        II. Others gainfully occupied, including em-
           ployers, traders and independent workers of
           all kinds.

        III. Housewives, that is, married women of
           working age.

IV. Others of working age not gainfully occupied.

V. Below working age.

VI. Retired above working age.

(iii) The sixth of these classes will receive retirement
pensions and the fifth will be covered by children's
allowances, which will be paid from the National
Exchequer in respect of all children when the
responsible parent is in receipt of insurance benefit
or pension, and in respect of all children except
one in other cases. The four other classes will be
insured for security appropriate to their circumstances. All classes will be covered for comprehensive medical treatment and rehabilitation and
for funeral expenses.

(iv) Every person in Class I, II or IV will pay a single
security contribution by a stamp on a single insurance document each week or combination of
weeks. In Class I the employer also will contribute, affixing the insurance stamp and deducting
the employee's share from wages or salary. The
contribution will differ from one class to another,
according to the benefits provided, and will be
higher for men than for women, so as to secure
benefits for Class III.

(v) Subject to simple contribution conditions, every
person in Class I will receive benefit for unemployment and disability, pension on retirement, medical
treatment and funeral expenses. Persons in Class II
will receive all these except unemployment benefit
and disability benefit during the first 13 weeks of
disability. Persons in Class IV will receive all these
except unemployment and disability benefit. As
a substitute for unemployment benefit, training
benefit will be available to persons in all classes

other than Class I, to assist them to find new
livelihoods if their present ones fail. Maternity
grant, provision for widowhood and separation
and qualification for retirement pensions will be
secured to all persons in Class III by virtue of
their husbands' contributions; in addition to
maternity grant, housewives who take paid work
will receive maternity benefit for 13 weeks to
enable them to give up working before and after
childbirth.

(vi) Unemployment benefit, disability benefit, basic
retirement pension after a transition period, and
training benefit will be at the same rate, irrespective of previous earnings. This rate will provide by itself the income necessary for subsistence
in all normal cases. There will be a joint rate for
a man and wife who is not gainfully occupied.
Where there is no wife or she is gainfully occupied,
there will be a lower single rate; where there is no
wife but a dependent above the age for childrens'
allowance, there will be a dependent allowance.
Maternity benefit for housewives who work also
for gain will be at a higher rate than the single
rate in unemployment or disability, while their
unemployment and disability benefit will be at a
lower rate; there are special rates also for widowhood as described below. With these exceptions all
rates of benefit will be the same for men and for
women. Disability due to industrial accident or
disease will be treated like all other disability for
the first 13 weeks; if disability continues thereafter, disability benefit at a flat rate will be replaced
by an industrial pension related to the earnings of
the individual, subject to a minimum and a
maximum.

(vii) Unemployment benefit will continue at the same

rate without means test so long as unemployment lasts, but will normally be subject to a condition of attendance at a work or training centre after a certain period. Disability benefit will continue at the same rate without means test, so long as disability lasts or till it is replaced by industrial pension, subject to acceptance of suitable medical treatment or vocational training.

(viii) Pensions (other than industrial) will be paid only on retirement from work. They may be claimed at any time after the minimum age of retirement, that is, 65 for men and 60 for women. The rate of pension will be increased above the basic rate if retirement is postponed. Contributory pensions as of right will be raised to the full basic rate gradually during a transition period of twenty years, in which adequate pensions according to needs will be paid to all persons requiring them. The position of existing pensioners will be safeguarded.

(ix) While permanent pensions will no longer be granted to widows of working age without dependent children, there will be for all widows a temporary benefit at a higher rate than unemployment or disability benefit, followed by training benefit where necessary. For widows with the care of dependent children there will be guardian benefit, in addition to the children's allowances, adequate for subsistence without other means. The position of existing widows on pension will be safeguarded.

(x) For the limited number of cases of need not covered by social insurance, national assistance subject to a uniform means test will be available.

(xi) Medical treatment covering all requirements will be provided for all citizens by a national health service organized under the health departments

and post-medical rehabilitation treatment will be provided for all persons capable of profiting by it.
(xii) A Ministry of Social Security will be established, responsible for social insurance, national assistance and encouragement and supervision of voluntary insurance and will take over, so far as necessary for these purposes, the present work of other Government departments and of Local Authorities in these fields.

The Plan thus summarized extends social insurance in four directions by bringing in, so far as possible and so far as their needs require it, all citizens and not only those employed under contract of service; by giving new benefits in cash, as for funerals, maternity and training, and in the form of comprehensive medical treatment and post-medical rehabilitation; by extending the period of benefit so as to make it, in the case of unemployment and disability, last as long as the need lasts; and by raising rates of benefit up to a level determined after examination of subsistence needs as sufficient to meet these needs in normal cases without other resources. The Plan is part of a policy of a national minimum.

The rates of benefit and contribution will depend to some extent on the cost of living when the Plan comes into force. On the assumption of a cost of living about 25 per cent above that of 1938, provisional rates of benefit and contribution are set out in paragraphs 401 and 403 of the Report. The most important of these. is a joint rate of 40/– a week for a man and wife in unemployment or disability and as retirement pension. The 40/– is for a man and a wife who is not herself gainfully occupied. For single men and women, or men whose wives are gainfully occupied, the rate is 24/–. There is a general maternity grant of £4 for all mothers and maternity benefit of 36/– a week for 13

weeks for women who are gainfully occupied. For prolonged disability resulting from industrial accident or
disease there will be industrial pension of two-thirds of
the earnings lost, subject to a minimum (of not being less
than would have been paid for ordinary disability) and
to a maximum of £3 a week. For widows there is a temporary benefit for 13 weeks at the same rate as maternity
benefit, that is to say 36/- a week, followed, if, and so
long as, the widow has dependent children, by a guardian
benefit of 24/- a week. All these benefits and pensions are
exclusive of allowances for dependent children at the rate
of 8/- for each child; it is proposed that these allowances
should be paid for every child when the responsible parent
is in receipt of any social insurance benefit or pension and
for every child but one in each family in other cases, i.e.
when the parent is earning.

The provisional rates mean that in unemployment or
disability a man and wife, if she is not working, with two
children, will receive 56/- a week without means test so
long as unemployment or disability lasts, as compared
with the 33/- in unemployment and the 15/- or 7/6 in
sickness with additional benefit in some approved societies
which they were getting before the war. In the case of
industrial disability a man with the same family will get
between 56/- and 76/- a week according to his earnings,
as compared with half earnings up to a maximum of 30/-
a week before the war and 43/- now.

In addition to social insurance, the Plan for Social
Security covers children's allowances, national assistance
and free comprehensive health and rehabilitation services.
The total cost of all these is estimated to amount to £697
millions in 1945, assumed as the first full year of the Plan,
and £858 millions twenty years after in 1965. These sums
include both present and new expenditure; the additional
charge on rates and taxes for all the purposes named above,
as compared with the present schemes, is put at £86

millions in 1945 and £254 millions in 1965. The contribution suggested is 7/6 a week in the case of an adult man in employment of which 4/3 will be paid by the man and 3/3 by the employer, and 6/– a week for an adult woman in employment of which 3/6 will be paid by the woman and 2/6 by the employer; there are lower contributions for non-adults, and for persons other than employees. It is estimated that, when the scheme is in full operation, the contributions of employees will provide about one-quarter of the total cost of their cash insurance benefits, exclusive of children's allowances and of national assistance, both of which will be provided wholly by taxation; the remaining three-quarters of the cash insurance benefits will be provided by taxation and the employers' contributions. In addition to the weekly contributions in insurance stamps, employers in industries scheduled as hazardous will pay an industrial levy towards the excess cost of accident and disease in those industries.

The Plan is based on the contributory principle of giving benefits as of right in return for contributions rather than free allowances from the State, of making contributions irrespective of the means of the contributor the basis of a claim to benefit irrespective of means. It accepts the view also that in social insurance organized by the State all men should stand in together on the same terms and that there should be no differentiation of contributions by risks except so far as separation of risks serves a social purpose (as it may do in relation to industrial accident and disease). In accord with this view of the nature of social insurance, the Report proposes supersession of the present system of approved societies giving unequal benefits for uniform compulsory contributions, of the exceptions from insurance accorded to particular occupations and of the special schemes of insurance in particular occupations. Ending of the approved society system is combined with a proposal to keep Friendly

Societies and Trade Unions which give sickness benefit as responsible agents for the administration of disability benefit.

The Report, while emphasizing the advantage to the citizen of unified and co-ordinated social insurance, points out that to obtain these advantages a number of changes are indispensable. Paragraph 30 of the Report gives a list of twenty-three changes, of which the following are the most important:

Change 4: Supersession of the present scheme of workmen's compensation and inclusion of provision for industrial accident or disease within the unified social insurance scheme subject to (*a*) a special method of meeting the cost of this provision, and (*b*) special pensions for prolonged disability and grants to dependents in cases of death due to such causes. This change turns the present system of workmen's compensation based on individual liability by employers and legal procedure into a social service. By making it part of the unified social insurance scheme it avoids demarcation difficulties, delays and duplication of machinery for raising funds and administering benefits. In place of throwing the whole cost of accidents in an industry on that particular industry, it shares the cost in part between different industries, on the ground that in social insurance different industries and individuals should stand in together. At the same time it recognizes the special character of disability due to industrial accident and disease, first by providing larger pensions where the disability is prolonged, and grants additional to the ordinary widowhood provision where death results; second, by raising part of the money through a special levy on employers in hazardous industries, designed to maintain an incentive for prevention of dangers. It is proposed that in each of the industries scheduled as hazardous, there should be statutory associations of employers and employees for the promotion of safety, rehabilitation and re-employment, for advice on regulations and for other purposes, including the allocation among individual employers of the total levy on each industry.

Change 6: Recognition of housewives as a distinct insurance class of occupied persons with benefits adjusted to their special needs, including (*a*) in all cases marriage grant, maternity grant, widowhood and separation provisions and retirement pensions; (*b*) if not gainfully occupied, benefit during husband's unemployment or disability; (*c*) if gainfully occupied, maternity benefit in addition to maternity grant. The Report emphasizes the vital task which housewives as mothers have to undertake in the next thirty years in ensuring the adequate continuance of the British race and gives to housewives as such, and not as dependents on their husbands, a share of the husband's unemployment or disability benefit, rights to maternity grant and benefit, widowhood and separation provisions and retirement pensions. For reasons set out in the Report it is proposed that housewives who are also gainfully occupied, while obtaining maternity benefit at a rate above the normal, should get unemployment and disability benefit at a lower rate than the normal, and that the Anomalies Regulations for Married Women should be abolished. In contrast to these Regulations, the Plan of the Report, taken as a whole, puts a premium on marriage, in place of penalizing it.

Change 14: Making of pensions, other than industrial, conditional on retirement from work and rising in value with each year of continued contribution after the minimum age of retirement, that is to say after 65 for men and 60 for women. The Report emphasizes the fact that, in view of the great and rapidly growing number of persons of pensionable age as compared with the total population, provision for age is the largest single problem in social insurance. It provides adequate pensions for all citizens as of right without means test, but makes this conditional upon retirement. In order to avoid hastening retirement from work, it increases the rate of pension for every year or postponement of retirement, that is to say of continued work and contribution after reaching the minimum age. It is proposed further that contributory pensions should rise to the full basic rate gradually over a transition period of twenty years. This transition will not affect any man now under the age of 45; those who being older are unable to qualify for the full contributory pensions will get substantial increases above the present rate of pension, and will be able to obtain assistance pensions on proof of need up to full subsistence level. The Report takes the view that, while the State must ultimately secure for all citizens adequate pensions as of right without means test in virtue of contributions, there can be no justification for giving full pensions forthwith to people who have neither contributed for them nor are in need of them. In adopting a transition period for adequate pensions with assistance pensions meanwhile for those who need them, the Plan for Britain follows the precedent of the Security Scheme of New Zealand.

Change 18: Inclusion of universal funeral grant in compulsory insurance. Meeting of the universal need for funeral expenses is a subject specially suitable for compulsory insurance and a need which can be met by such insurance far more cheaply than by the present system of voluntary insurance. In view both of the possible effect of this proposal and the change in regard to approved societies upon the business of industrial assurance, and of the criticisms in regard to industrial assurance made by former committees of inquiry, the Report proposes that the business of industrial assurance should be converted

into a public service under an Industrial Assurance
Board.

Change 19: Transfer to the Ministry of Social Security
of the remaining functions of Local Authorities in respect
of public assistance, other than treatment and services of
an institutional character. The Report envisages close
co-operation between the Ministry of Social Security with
its decentralized organization and the Local Authorities,
responsibilities being divided on the basis that provision
of cash payments is the primary function of the Ministry
and that provision of institutional treatment and services
is the primary responsibility of the Local Authority. In
addition to public assistance it is proposed that responsibility for the maintenance of blind persons should be
transferred on the same lines to the Ministry of Social
Security and that the Ministry should frame a new scheme
for maintenance and welfare by co-operation between the
Ministry, local authorities and voluntary agencies. It is
pointed out in the Report that most persons who become
blind nowadays do so after a period of working life and
when the insurance scheme is in operation will have
acquired rights to permanent disability benefit.

While giving this long list of changes, the Report
emphasizes the fact that all its proposals are based on
experience of the existing schemes and retain their essential features. In particular, the Plan retains the contributory
principle of sharing the cost of security between three
parties, the insured person, his employer if he has an
employer, and the State. It retains and extends the principle
(which distinguishes British social insurance from the
schemes of most other countries) that compulsory insurance should provide a flat rate of benefit irrespective of
earnings in return for a flat contribution from all. It
retains as the best method of contribution the system of
insurance documents and stamps. It provides for retain-

ing on a new basis the association of Friendly Societies with national health insurance. It provides for retaining within the general framework of a unified scheme some of the special features of workmen's compensation and for converting the associations for mutual indemnity in industries chiefly concerned into new organs of industrial co-operation and self-government. The scheme of the Report is in some ways a revolution, but in more important ways it is a natural development from the past. It is a British revolution.

The Plan for Social Security is put forward as something which should, if possible, be in force as soon as the war ends. To secure this it is necessary that a decision of principle should be taken in the near future. It is put forward as a measure necessary to translate the words of the Atlantic Charter into deeds. It is put forward as part of a concerted social policy attacking not Want only, but the four other evils of Disease (by development of health services for prevention and cure); of Ignorance (by development of education); of Squalor (by better planning of the location of industry and population and by housing); and of Idleness (by maintenance of employment and prevention of mass unemployment). The last of these objects, namely maintenance of employment, is described as one of the assumptions underlying the Plan for Social Security, without whose realization much that might otherwise be gained through the plan will be wasted.

The Report is divided into six parts, of which Part I, giving an introduction and summary of the whole, and Part VI, placing social security in relation to social policy and discussing the abolition of want as a practicable postwar aim, are of most general interest. Part II gives the reasons for each of the principal changes proposed, and Part III examines three problems of special difficulty, including that of the benefit rates required for subsistence and the problem of age, while Part IV deals with the Social

Security Budget, that is to say the expenditure involved and the means of meeting it. The Plan for Social Security is set out in detail in Part V. A Memorandum by the Government Actuary dealing with the financial aspects of the Plan is attached in an Appendix (A). There are other appendices giving a survey of the existing schemes (B), naming the organizations which gave evidence (C), and dealing respectively with the problem of industrial assurance (D), with the administrative costs of different types of insurance (E) and with some principal points of comparison with the social insurance methods of countries other than Britain (F). Memoranda submitted by a number of the organizations giving evidence are printed separately in Appendix G.

The financial effects of the Plan are shown in two tables attached, one (Table XII) giving the estimated social security expenditure in 1945 and 1965, and the other (Table XIV) comparing the security provision made under the Plan for a man, wife and two children of the present contributory classes, with the provision made for such a family before the war.

The Report concludes:

"Freedom from want cannot be forced on a democracy or given to a democracy. It must be won by them. Winning it needs courage and faith and a sense of national unity: courage to face facts and difficulties and overcome them: faith in our future and in the ideals of fair play and freedom for which century after century our forefathers were prepared to die: a sense of national unity overriding the interests of any class or section. The Plan for Social Security in this Report is submitted by one who believes that in this supreme crisis the British people will not be found wanting in courage and faith and national unity, in material and spiritual power to play their part in achieving both social security and the victory of justice among nations upon which security depends."

TABLE XII

ESTIMATED SOCIAL SECURITY EXPENDITURE 1945 AND 1965

	1945 £ millions	1965 £ millions
Social Insurance —		
Unemployment Benefit (including training benefit)	110	107
Disability Benefit other than industrial	57	71
Industrial Disability Benefit, Pensions and Grant..	15	15
Retirement Pensions..	126	300
Widows' and Guardian Benefit	29	21
Maternity Grant and Benefit	7	6
Marriage Grant	1	3
Funeral Grant	4	12
Cost of Administration	18	18
Total Social Insurance	367	553
National Assistance —		
Assistance Pensions	39	25
Other Assistance.	5	5
Cost of Administration	3	2
Children's Allowances	110	100
Cost of Administration	3	3
Health and Rehabilitation Services	170	170
TOTAL	697	858

TABLE XIV

SECURITY PROVISION FOR MAN, WIFE AND TWO CHILDREN

(Present Contributory Classes)

	Pre-War*		Proposed in Plan for Social Security	
	Amount	Period and Conditions	Amount	Period and Conditions
Unemployment ..	33/- per week.	26 weeks (followed by assistance on means test).	56/- per week.	Unlimited in time without means test at any time. Subject to attendance at a training centre if unemployment is prolonged.
Disability other than industrial	15/- per week.	26 weeks, followed by 7/6 per week in disablement. Additional benefit in some cases.	56/- per week.	Unlimited in time without means test at any time.
Old Age	20/- per week.	—	40/- per week.	On retirement, 2/- a week increase for each year of postponement of retirement. (Full rate only after transition period. Assistance pensions on means test meanwhile).
Widowhood ..	18/- per week.	—	40/- per week.	Reduced by part of any earnings. 52/- per week for first thirteen weeks without reduction.

Maternity	£2	—	£4	—
Maternity if wife gainfully occupied	£2 additional.	—	36/- per week for 13 weeks additional.	—
Funeral	Nil.	—	£20	With smaller sums for children.
Industrial Disability	Half earnings up to maximum of 30/- per week.	Subject to compounding for lump sums.	56/- p.w. for 13 weeks, followed by pension of two-thirds earnings up to maximum of 76/-p.w., but not less than 56/- p.w. No compounding for total disability.	—
Medical Treatment	General Practitioner for man with additional treatment benefits in some cases.	—	Comprehensive medical treatment, including hospital, dental and ophthalmic, nursing and convalescent homes for whole family. Post-medical rehabilitation.	—

* Some of the pre-war rates of benefit shown above have been revised in the course of the present war. At the date of the Report the benefit in unemployment was 5/- higher than that shown, and that for disability was 3/- higher. For industrial disability, the pre-war maximum of 30/- has been raised to 35/-, and children's allowances of 4/- for each of the first two children and 3/- for subsequent children have been added. For pensions the pensionable age in the case of women has been lowered from 65 to 60. With these changes the contributions for unemployment, health and pensions were raised, so that the total contribution by an adult man in 1942 was 1/10 in place of 1/7 in 1938.

8

FOUR QUESTIONS ON THE PLAN*

THE Plan for Social Security set out in my Report aims
at the abolition of physical Want by provision of a minimum income at all times. It involves a re-distribution of
income both vertically and horizontally by insurance contributions. Today I shall try to answer four main questions
that may be asked about the Plan.

(i) *Will such a Plan sap individuality and adventure?*

No, for the adventurous are those who have been well-
fed; it wasn't starved people who founded either the
British Commonwealth or the United States of America.
No, for there is no ceiling to human enterprise or needs;
if everyone is assured of £2 a week for himself and his
wife in old age, nearly everyone will want to be better
off, and will feel safe in trying to save for this, if there is
no means test. No, for if the State does something for all
children, that won't stop parents from trying to do better
than others for their particular children. Man is a spirit,
not an animal.

(ii) *Can we afford it?*

Can we afford to do without it? Re-distribution of
income does not abolish Want, unless there is enough in
total. There was ample in total before this war, in spite of
the last war and its destructive aftermath. There will be
ample in total after this war if we can use our productive
resources in productive employment. But if there were
not going to be plenty, my Plan would be needed even

* Points from Address at Savoy Hotel, 9th December, 1942 (See Note 8).

more—to make the best use of what we had, by putting the most urgent needs first.

(iii) *Will this Plan take us half-way to Moscow or to New York?*

I am glad to say, neither. Geographically neither, for half-way to Moscow lands us near Berlin and half-way to New York is the mid-Atlantic.

Seriously neither, for as a social insurance scheme this is built wholly on British lines, not like anything in other countries, particularly unlike both the Russian and the American schemes.

Seriously neither, for the Plan is a move neither towards Socialism nor towards Capitalism. It goes straight down the middle of the road between them to a practical end. It is needed in any form of economic organization.

Finally, the Plan raises no party issues. Social insurance is not a party preserve. The Conservatives took the first step towards Social Security in one special field—that of Industrial accident—by the Workmen's Compensation Act of 1897. The Liberals laid the foundation of our present system with non-contributory pensions in 1908 and health and unemployment insurance in 1911. The Conservatives brought in contributory pensions including widows and orphans in 1925. I was put on to my present job by two Ministers of the Labour Party—Mr. Greenwood and Mr. Bevin.

(iv) *If this Plan is adopted, is that all that is needed?*

Of course not. In addition to Want, there are four other giant evils named in the Report that must be attacked as part of a concerted campaign.

Of course not. We have to win this war—we have not done so yet. We can neglect no effort, nothing that brings unity among allies or puts heart into our people. That last need is a reason for planning peace even in war.

When I was asked in June, 1941, to take the Chairmanship of the Inter-Departmental Committee on Social Insurance and Allied Services, I felt frankly a little sad. I
wanted to do something directly helping the war and I
thought that there were things that I could do. Each one
of us thinks that he can poke the fire a little better than
the other fellow. I wanted a hand in poking the fire of
war.

I did hardly anything about social insurance for the
first four or five months—devoting my time to the Committee on Skilled Men in the Services. I was even rather
glad later to turn from social insurance for a month or so
to explore fuel rationing; whether that can be described
as poking the fire of war, I'm not sure.

Gradually, as I got deeper into social insurance, I came
to realize the intense interest of the citizens of this country
in the problem of security after the war. I had a lesson in
democracy, and of what is needed to make a democracy
whole-hearted in war. Democracies make war for peace
not war for its own sake. They fight better if they know
what they are fighting for after the war. Those of us who
have our futures assured, or have no futures or no children,
may be content to fight for victory over the enemy. Once
that is secured, the present system "will last our time."
But it won't last the time of the British race.

Interest in security after the war is not just the selfish
interest of men desiring benefit for themselves. It is also
expression of a desire to make a better world for others—
for all—by democratic means.

I make one last point: this is a Plan on British lines. It
is a Plan for security with responsibilities and freedom. It
is a Plan imaginative but practical. It is a Plan for Britain,
but not a Plan to help Britain at the expense of others. It
represents not national selfishness but a contribution to
the common cause of all the United Nations whose aim
is the happiness of the common man.

TRANSFORMATION SCENE

"Avaunt, foul sprite! and be no-longer seen:
I'll have you know I am the Fairy Queen!"

Reproduced by permission of the Proprietors of "Punch"

9

NEW BRITAIN*

THOUGH I am the author of a Report on Social Insurance and Allied Services, I am not today going to speak in any detail at all about that Report, and not indeed mainly about that Report. For that there are two reasons. One reason is that I am the author. I have just spilt about one hundred and ten thousand words into print on Social Insurance and Allied Services. There's really a good deal more than this number of words—there are about another fifty thousand of Appendix. I have a feeling that I ought to sit back for a time and let the other fellows have a say before I say more upon this subject. But the real reason, the second and greater reason why I have taken for my subject today New Britain rather than my Report, is that there are so many larger and more difficult problems to solve in the peace and after the war than this particular problem to which my Report is devoted. I shall be able to show that in a moment.

I have taken as my text for my address, the words "New Britain". I believe those two words are as good a short motto as one can find for all that one wants to do in post-war reconstruction. Most people want something new after the war. Very few of us want something utterly unlike the Britain that we have known and loved. Some people normally put the emphasis on *New* Britain. Others, generally a little older, put the emphasis on New *Britain*. Some people put the emphasis one way if they have got up rather bad-tempered in the morning or haven't been doing very well, and they put the emphasis the other way when they've had a successful day. Some people shift the emphasis from time to time, and as they shift the emphasis

* Address at Oxford, 6th December, 1942.

they shift votes and power between the political parties, between those parties which are emphasizing change and those which are emphasizing the keeping of Britain. New Britain sums up the common desires of all of us today, of those who emphasize the *New* and those who emphasize the *Britain*.

New Britain as a motto for post-war aims has other implications also. It means that, in planning the world after the war, we in Britain should look first to putting our own house in order and dealing with things which are within our power, before we try to put the whole world in order, before we advise other countries how they should manage their colour problem or their colonial problem or any other problem; that we should put our house in order and make the kind of world in which our own people should live. That does not mean of course that Britain should have no concern with the rest of the world. For three hundred years Britain has been an important power and, on the whole, a power for good in the world and will go on being that in the future. I shall come back to international problems before I finish today.

FREEDOM FROM FIVE GIANT EVILS

But in the first instance I am concerned with asking— What kind of Britain do we want at home? In what shall New Britain differ most definitely from the old Britain that we have known? I phrase that difference to myself— I've said this before—chiefly by saying that New Britain should be free, as free as is humanly possible, of the five giant evils, of Want, of Disease, of Ignorance, of Squalor and of Idleness.

Freedom from Want is the aim of the Report on Social Insurance and Allied Services which I have just made to the Government and which they have just published. That Report is now before Government, Parliament and the

nation, and, because I want to talk of other things chiefly,
I shall say relatively little about it here today. I'll only say
this: that all the proposals that I have made are part of a
policy of a national minimum of income. You can't abolish
Want unless you make sure that everybody willing to
work, everybody subject to occasional accidents and mis-
fortunes that interrupt his earning, has at all times, for all
his responsibilities, the income necessary to meet those
responsibilities. Abolition of Want means a national minimum and that national minimum mustn't be and can't be
simply a minimum wage when a man is working—when
he's earning, because there are times when men cannot
work and cannot earn: when they are unemployed (there
must always be some unemployment in a changing society),
when they are sick, when they are old, when they are
damaged by accident, when the bread-winner dies. If you
want to abolish Want you must provide a minimum
income as of right, without any question of other means,
a minimum income as of right to meet those inevitable
interruptions of earnings. That, in a sentence, is the point
of all those many words which I've written about the
Social Insurance Scheme in my Report. It's a means of
taking some of the national income—the income of all the
men and women of this country, when they are earning—
and keeping it for the times when some of them cannot
earn.

But social insurance alone, giving an income to people
when their earning power is interrupted, will not abolish
Want, because it will not always provide the necessary
income for all urgent needs. It will not do that nor will a
minimum wage do it. It's no use, for instance, to lay down
a minimum wage and say this is the minimum wage,
enough for a man and wife and two children or three
children, because there will be some families with four and
five and six children—and unless there are many families
with large numbers of children, the British race will not

continue. We haven't now anything like enough children being born to keep our race in being. If you want to abolish Want, you must add to your minimum wage legislation, and to your social insurance for interruption of earnings— you must add children's allowances. That is part of my scheme: children's allowances paid both when the responsible parent is earning and when the responsible parent is not earning. You must add also provision for those expenses which come when children are being born, at maternity; that is part of the Social Insurance Scheme.

PREVENTION OF WANT THE FIRST STEP

Well now, that's all I'm going to say about this scheme of my Report. You must conceive of it as an attempt to secure freedom from Want, by seeing that everyone at all times, in virtue of contributions made by him, and as of right without any means tests, has the minimum income necessary to meet his responsibilities. If when you say freedom from Want you mean it, and don't just mean a pious platitude, you will have to adopt, not necessarily my precise scheme, but something like this scheme, something that does all the things that this scheme does. If you can find another way of doing them, I don't mind. But something like it is needed if you want freedom from Want. And that is the basis of all our post-war reconstruction—the first step to take.

But it is only the first step. Let me come on to those other giant evils that I have named. One is Disease. Well, Disease is also, to some extent, dealt with in my Report, because my Report proposes that there shall be a comprehensive medical service covering every kind of treatment at home and in hospital—dental, ophthalmic, general, specialist, consultant, nursing services, everything—covering that without a charge at the time of treatment, in virtue of a contribution made and included in the weekly contribution which the Social Insurance Scheme proposes. We can't of course abolish all Disease, but here again the principle of the national minimum applies. We ought to regard it as part of the national minimum for every citizen that he should be as well as science applied to the prevention and cure of Disease can make him. That is the medical side of my proposals and of the national minimum.

In regard to the giant Disease my Report says something. It provides the money or shows where you can get the money for dealing with this problem by a comprehensive medical service. But it doesn't go into the method of how you should organize the medical service, how you should control and finance voluntary hospitals, how you should pay and employ doctors. That's a very big problem of organization which had to be left out of my Report because I couldn't have written it by this Christmas if I'd had to deal with it. It will have to be tackled afterwards. You may say that my Report deals with the whole of the problem of freedom from Want, and about half of the problem of Disease.

DEALING WITH IGNORANCE

I come now to those three other evils: Ignorance, Squalor, Idleness. Dealing with Ignorance means, of course, the development of education. It means more and better schools. It means, no doubt, a raising of the school age. It means giving greater opportunity—greater equality of education—to all children, irrespective of their class or family circumstances. It means that for two reasons: first, that no community can afford to waste any of its talent; second, and this is an equally good human reason, that any wasted talent is a source of unhappiness. The people who are being employed below their capacity are the unhappy ones, and we want to abolish that cause of unhappiness as well as use their talents.

But dealing with Ignorance isn't only—I'm not sure that it's even mainly—a question regarding young people. All of us old people are very ignorant of many things which we ought to know. I believe that adult education on a greatly extended scale is almost as important as, if not more important than, more education of the young. There are really many things that you learn better when you are older, when you are out in the world. And I hope we shan't concentrate on just pumping more education into the young. We should insist on pumping more knowledge of the world at large, of politics, of history, of economics and all the rest of it, into our adult citizens.

To lay plans for our educational development is the third of our tasks. I have no time today to say much about this task. The main thing I would say is that the proper timing of our educational measures is essential. Look at what the position is going to be immediately after this war, in which we haven't been educating the necessary teachers; they've been fighting or doing urgent war work. We shall find an acute shortage of teachers. Frankly, I don't want to see an enormous mass of additional pupils brought into schools until we are certain that we can teach them better, until we have enough teachers and good enough teachers, to do not merely as well as we've been doing before, but better. The main problem at the moment is to make certain that we're going to have good teaching and enough teachers after the war. That's all I would say about that third task of dealing with Ignorance.

DEALING WITH SQUALOR

I come to my fourth giant—Squalor. What do I mean by Squalor? I mean the bad living conditions which arise from the fact that we do not plan our towns or our countryside, how cities shall grow, where our factories shall be placed, where our houses shall be placed. We do not have proper planning of the use of the land for the people to work in and to live in. Apart from that I mean that we haven't now anything like enough houses or good enough houses. Dealing with Squalor means planning town and countryside and having many more and better houses. We've had a number of Reports dealing with various sides of this question of planning the location of industry and planning the use of land. We've had the Barlow Report just before the war, or at the beginning of the war, and the Scott Report and the Uthwatt Report— and they have been of great value in showing some of the problems. But I think it's clear that we haven't yet in this country strong enough machinery to secure the proper distribution of industry and population over our country. Exactly what we ought to do, I don't know. This is a point on which I begin to raise questions rather than to answer them. It's very difficult to say what powers you need to determine how land shall be used, and when you begin to exercise that power, you get into very difficult questions of rights of property and value and compensation for interference with the use of land, and so on and so on. Beyond that, if you're going to deal with Squalor, you've got a problem of regulating your transport facilities. Finally, we're going to have an immense task of reorganizing the whole of the building trade, so that it is equal to the heavy task that is going to fall upon it after the war. Here is a very difficult problem which we haven't, I think, yet even begun to get down to seriously—I don't mean we haven't done something. Many enquiries are being made, but there is a great unconquered evil of Squalor in our towns and countryside which we must learn to conquer.

I come now to the fifth of the evils from which I wish to see the country free, and we must all wish to see the country free—and that is the giant evil of Idleness, that is to say, of mass-unemployment. I don't believe that we need aim at getting rid of all unemployment in this country any more than we can get rid of all disease. A certain amount of unemployment can be properly dealt with by unemployment insurance, by giving a man an income while he is doing nothing. But to give a man an income while he is doing nothing—not for a few weeks or even a few months, but for years and years—is an entire misuse of the whole idea of unemployment insurance.

PREVENTION OF MASS-UNEMPLOYMENT VITAL

Somehow or other to prevent recurrence of mass-unemployment prolonged for years and years, such as we experienced between the first World War and the present World War, is the most important, the most difficult and most urgent of all the tasks which we have to consider today. It's the most important in itself, because unless we can avoid mass-unemployment, all else that we can do is futile. If we can avoid mass-unemployment, there's going to be no difficulty at all about paying for my scheme of social insurance in my Report and for all other essential social reforms. But if we cannot avoid mass-unemployment, if we have a large part of the people doing nothing, then we may not be able to afford it, or we may not be able to afford it in a way in which we really keep the people from Want. We may pay them so much in money, but there will not be enough goods being produced for that money, and they will not be out of Want. It's most important in itself, this abolition of mass-unemployment or prevention of mass-unemployment. It is also the most important of all the tasks psychologically, because everyone of us knows that the anxiety that is at the back of most people's minds in this country today is a fear of going back to something like what happened between the two wars.

That fear is the disturbing anxiety of all those who

in the war have given up their former work, whether to
go into the Forces or to do any other kind of work: they
don't know what they're coming back to. Most important
of all reconstruction problems on the home front is this
task of dealing with mass-unemployment. It is also perhaps
the most difficult. I do not know—and being an academic
person I'm not going to say I know before I think I
know—I know I do not now know just how to solve the
problem of maintaining productive employment after the
war. All I can say is that I refuse to believe that it is
insoluble. When people tell me that we cannot abolish
unemployment, I say that we have abolished unemployment twice in my lifetime—in the last war and in this war.
I don't know how far it is absolutely true, but it is very
nearly true, that in Russia they have abolished unemployment or at least they have no scheme of unemployment
insurance. Now, I simply do not believe that it is impossible
to abolish unemployment in Britain, but I do not yet know
exactly how it ought to be done, and I don't know
whether anybody yet knows how it ought to be done.

That is why I call this problem perhaps the most difficult. It is very difficult. It is at the same time extremely
urgent, because if we are to maintain employment after
the war, to find a use for all our labour—to change over
the people who are now making the munitions of war into
making what will be equally wanted—the munitions of peace
and all that we need in peace—we must make the plans for
that now: it's no good waiting until after the war to make
the plans. Preparing to prevent Idleness is an urgent task.

Finally, this task may prove to be the most contro-
versial. It does raise directly the question of how much
further the State may need to enter into the economic
sphere: of how much further in the direction either of
Socialism or of planning or of something of that sort, we
may need to go: of what are to be the relations between
the State and private enterprise in the future. That, unfor-

tunately, is one of the issues which are apt to divide political parties, as most of the other problems I have mentioned do not divide them. There's no party question at all about dealing with Want by social insurance; all parties would accept the principle of a national minimum and accept the principle of securing it by social insurance. There's no party question about Ignorance, about more education, or about dealing with Disease. There are difficult party questions with regard to ownership of land and the rights of property in dealing with Squalor, but they are not central to the problem. But when you come to this last problem of all—the maintaining of productive employment—you get into a region in which the policy of the country and the sentiment of the country aren't yet settled and agreed. That's why it is so necessary to discuss that problem, to see if by discussion we cannot reach agreement. In this Britain of ours, we are in fact all so sufficiently near to one another, that by discussion we can get to agreement on most things; discussion of this problem of maintaining productive employment is one of our most urgent duties today.

All Five Tasks Essential

From this review of the five evils whose absence or diminution should distinguish New Britain from the old, you will see why I spoke of the relative unimportance of social insurance. I don't under-estimate the value of the need for a minimum income for all times. But to provide that is only one of the five tasks and it's the easiest, because we're all agreed in principle and we're very nearly agreed on the methods. Until all the other tasks are taken in hand, I shall, for my part, put the emphasis on "new" and say that I want a *new* Britain rather than a new *Britain*. I shall want to see change, and you, I think, will all want to see change, until all five problems are dealt with seriously.

Three Strategic Principles

How should we approach those five tasks? I've no full answer to that question today. First of all I should have to study for many months and then talk for a month if I was to attempt to give full answers to all these questions. I am only going to lay down three general principles that today seem to me important in approaching the solution of these post-war problems; they are the three strategic principles of our campaign to win New Britain. The first principle is that whatever else we do there are certain essential British liberties which we must preserve. There are certain things which if we destroy, I should say we were not in New Britain, but in new somewhere else. Those—to me—essential British liberties include freedom of worship, freedom of speech, writing, study and teaching, freedom of association and making of new parties of every kind, freedom of choice of occupation, and freedom of spending a personal income. Without these freedoms Britain to me would not be Britain and I would go somewhere else, however new it was.

Having said that I go to the second principle. Subject to any limits set by the need to preserve these essential liberties, we ought to be prepared to use the powers of the State so far as may be necessary without any limit whatever, in order to abolish those five giant evils. Those freedoms I have named are essential, but no established interests are essential, no particular methods of production are essential. All these must, if necessary, be sacrificed to secure destruction of those five giants.

The third general principle is that if the power of the State is to be used in new fields for new purposes one must be prepared if necessary to make changes in the machinery of Government. Those are my three general principles for planning the campaign against the five giants. First, certain liberties are essential and must be preserved in any case. Second, subject to preservation of these liberties one must be prepared to use the powers of the State so far as necessary. Third, one must be prepared to change the machinery of Government so far as necessary for the performance of new tasks.

Let me make it clear that saying that the machinery of Government must be changed if necessary doesn't mean changing everything—making changes which aren't necessary. So saying that certain liberties are essential and must be kept at all costs doesn't mean that nothing else need be kept or will be kept. I don't want unnecessary change—change for the sake of change. Thus, though I do not regard any particular political device as essential, provided that I am sure of those essential liberties, I also do not believe that there is any need for changing the major part of our political institutions. When I name five or six essential liberties, I don't mean that they're the only things that will survive from the old Britain into the new. Many things will survive, and for my part I hope that the present Parliamentary system, with parties and the power to form new parties, with something of the present relation between Government and Parliament, and of members representing citizens in general will continue. In relation to Parliament, I'm inclined to be rather conservative, to say New *Britain*, rather than to try new forms of election, such as the indirect or Soviet system or representation of particular functions or interests, like councils of industry. I don't believe that we need any other type of assembly, other than this old British Parliament that we have known. We often amuse ourselves by saying rude things about Parliament and its members, but Parliament today gives the one absolutely essential condition of democracy.

THE ESSENTIAL CONDITION OF DEMOCRACY

The essential part of democracy to me is not that I should spend a lot of time in governing myself, for I have many more amusing things to do. But I want to be quite certain that I can change the person who governs me without having to shoot him. That is the essence of Democracy, that you can have a peaceful change of governors without shooting. To me a country is not a Democracy, whatever else it may be and whatever other virtues it may have, if you cannot change the Government by a perfectly peaceful method of putting your cross on a piece of paper. Well, Parliament gives us that every five years, and that is all I want from Parliament really, though it can do a lot of other things as well.

But saying that Parliament should continue, doesn't mean that we want no change of Government machinery. If, for instance, we want to maintain employment in this country, one thing we have to do is to make a design of how all the productive resources of a country—all the men and the women and the factories and the skill in it—can be used after the war in meeting needs which we know will exist. That is what is called national planning, making a design as to how these resources could be used so as to produce the things that we need. Well, now it is quite certain that there is not now in this country any part of the existing machine of government capable of making such a design. The body that I look to to make such a design is what I call an Economic General Staff, somebody to plan our economic life—to make a plan for economic readjustment after the war—just as a military general staff plans a campaign. How the plan is to be carried out—whether it's to be carried out by the State or by private enterprise—is another question. The first step is that somebody has to make the plan. There is no one now to make the plan, and we want what I call an Economic General Staff to do it.

Apart from that special requirement of an Economic General Staff to plan our economic campaign, if the State is going to do a great many more things in the economic sphere, and I'm fairly sure it will have to do a great many more things in the economic sphere, we want—not necessarily better people than the present Civil Servants—but different types of people and different types of training and different types of organization. I think it's essential that all those who press for extension of the State's activity should realize that this means changing the machinery of the State to some extent.

A Positive Moral Aim

So far I have defined New Britain rather negatively by naming five evils which should be destroyed. You may ask whether I can't find a positive aim. Is there no moral purpose for the British community, and for the British individual?

Well, I think one can name it as a positive aim for the British community, that it should take the task of reconciling this security which we have not had in the past, with retention of the individual liberty and responsibility which we have had in the past, but which are threatened in some countries in the name of security. For the individual we can't find a moral aim as it is found in Germany, by subordinating the individual to the State, and by raising the State to Godhead. The essence of Britain, old and new, is that the individual is more than the State, and is the object for which the State exists. There must be as many separate aims as there are separate lives in the State. But perhaps a single common purpose may be found for all by saying that in every individual life there should be the ideal—what some people would call the sense of a Divine vocation—the ideal of doing something in his daily life which is not for his personal gain, or even for the personal gain of his own family—something which is done consciously by him as a member of a community, as a member of his local community, as a member of the nation, as a member of the brotherhood of man.

One of the weaknesses of many reformers in the past is that they have not taken account sufficiently of the immense feeling of patriotism in the British people, of that loving pride which we have in our country. It's often been said that the worker has no country. That has never been true of British workers and never will be. We have a loving pride in our country. It is in serving our country that most of us can find that aim outside our personal gain which we need in our lives—in peace as in war.

NEW BRITAIN NOT ISOLATIONIST

I speak of patriotism and of serving Britain, but of course to take New Britain as one's motto is not to be an isolationist in the world. Dealing with the last of those five giants, unemployment, will in any case involve making many new economic relations with other countries. Much more than that, New Britain in the new world, like old Britain, will be one of the family of all nations. Britain can't be thought of apart from the British Commonwealth or the United Nations with whom we are waging this war. We must all share in the task which will arise after the war, of exploring and defining the meaning of national trusteeship after the war. What do I mean by national trusteeship? Well, there are certain powers which we with the other United Nations will have to exercise after the war in the interests of order. We shall have, I hope, all the armed force that there is in the world when this war ends. We must show ourselves able to use armed force, not for the special advantage of British or American or Russian citizens, but as trustees for the common good of mankind.

That is what I mean by national trusteeship, in the use of the armed force which must remain in the world if the world is to remain at peace. There's another field in which too the need for exploring and defining and giving effect to the idea of trusteeship is vital. There are certain parts of the world which are not yet able or fit to govern themselves from within, for various reasons; I needn't go into them. Well, my view is that every part of the world should either be governed from within, and that to me means democratically, or if it is governed with force from without, that government must be in the interest of the community which is governed and in no other interest whatever. That is national trusteeship in the government of colonial territory. We have in this country a long and honourable tradition of movement towards that ideal. I reject for my part the criticism that we are ignorant of that ideal or haven't had it before us. But there's much to be done in making it more universal, in applying it throughout the world. Whenever any part of the earth is governed not from within it should be treated as the beneficiary of a trust is treated; the trust must be administered for his good and not to the advantage of the trustee.

Finally, immediately after the war ends, even if Want is abolished in this island, as I think it can be abolished by a combination of maintenance of employment and of social insurance, even if want is abolished here, there'll be bitter Want in many countries which will not have escaped, as Britain has hitherto escaped and will, we hope, continue to escape, destruction by the war. Clearly we must look forward to great responsibilities in giving the first aid that will be needed in Europe and many other countries immediately after this war is over.

FINDING AGREEMENT BY DISCUSSION

I've tried to put before you the magnitude and the difficulty of the problems that face us. To do so is not to suggest that they're insoluble. I've done so in the hope of helping to prepare the way for a solution by discussion.

I'm an academic person: I don't find it easy to speak with
certainty unless I feel sure, and I do not know yet with
certainty, what is the remedy for those evils of Squalor
and Idleness. But being an academic person means also
being one who believes in the persuasive power of reason.
As an academic person who lives by selling reason, I
believe that in this eminently reasonable British community, sufficient discussion always leads ultimately to
agreement.

One of the reasons why after winning the last war we
lost all its fruits, was that during the war itself, there
wasn't sufficient general discussion or forming of public
opinion as to what should happen after. We all thought
rather vaguely of going back to the good old days. This
time we all know we can't go back to the old days because
they weren't good enough, with their mass unemployment
and economic wars and breeding of new military wars.
We must go forward to something better than the old
days. The reception that has been given to my Report
shows that the people of this country are intensely
interested and rightly interested now in making up their
minds by discussion as to what should happen after the
war to get a New Britain better than the old Britain. That
is an admirable sign; what is most needed is informed
discussion of all the problems that I've put before you.

WAR AND PEACE INDIVISIBLE

I've been talking only of the New Britain after the war.
To talk of that is not to neglect the war itself. Victory in
war and victory in peace are really indivisible. To ensure
victory in this war, the United Nations, for all their
immense resources, must strain every nerve. They must
secure from every one of their citizens the utmost of his
personal effort and last ounce of individual effort. To
secure that in democracies like ours—from a nation of free

men loving peace—we must set aims for war which appeal to such men and will be approved by them. Democracies, like Cromwell's armies, must know what they fight for and love what they know.

The German tyrant has taken as his motto the 'New Order', the spreading by force of German ideas over subject peoples. That is all very well for a tyrant man and a tyrant race. It's idle as a watchword for democracy. How could such a phrase stir the blood of common men who love their fellows? The phrase which to me sums up briefly that for which we in this nation should fight, is New Britain as I have tried to explain it. For each of our Allies it can be the same—New Poland, New America, New Russia, New France. And in the end—even New Germany. All should be lands where common men shall be secure with freedom. I ask you to take for your motto New Britain, as something to be realized not by quarrelling but by taking thought; by taking thought not in the aftermath of war but now; by discussing not abstractions but a series of concrete problems, of specific evils, of Want, Disease, Ignorance, Squalor, Idleness, to be attacked by a concerted campaign; by finding through reason the way to solve our problems as well as having the will to do it. To win this war will tax all our strength, courage and staying power, and the strength, courage and staying power of our Allies. To solve in advance at the same time the main problems of the peace, will tax to the utmost our imagination, our intelligence and our good-will. But both things have to be done. Let's do them. There are no easy times ahead in this war or in the peace. Which of you has asked for an easy time?

10

THE PILLARS OF SECURITY*

I.—The Assumption of Employment

In the Report which I made to His Majesty's Government on Social Insurance and Allied Services, I expressed the view that no satisfactory scheme of Social Security could be devised except on three assumptions:

A. Children's allowances, paid both when the responsible parent is earning and when he is not earning.

B. Comprehensive health and rehabilitation services for prevention and cure of disease and restoration of capacity for work, available to all members of the community.

C. Maintenance of employment, that is to say, avoidance of mass unemployment.

Assumption A, of children's allowances, is an integral part of the security scheme for redistribution of income according to needs: without it freedom from want cannot be obtained. The main practical questions with regard to children's allowances, including their form, amount, source and method of administration, are dealt with accordingly in the Report itself.

Assumption B, of comprehensive health and rehabilitation services, falls partly within and partly without the scope of the Report, and is dealt with in the Report only in so far as provision is made for meeting part of the cost involved from insurance contributions. The many important problems that arise as to the organization of the

* *Observer*, 3rd, 10th, 17th, and 24th January, 1943. *Daily Herald*, 23rd, 25th, 26th, and 28th January, 1943.

health and rehabilitation services, in seeking to realize this assumption, are left over for further inquiry.

Assumption C, of the maintenance of employment, though essential to give full value to the proposals in the Report, has been treated as falling wholly outside its scope. For that reason, while the Report itself is under consideration by the Government and by Parliament, it may be helpful and proper to say something more about Assumption C and to show the relation between this assumption and the Plan for Social Security contained in the Report. This will be done here. What is the meaning of Assumption C? Why is this assumption regarded as an essential basis for Social Security? Is the assumption reasonable in itself?

In the course of this examination it will appear that there is yet a fourth assumption of Social Security after the war, as much outside the scope of the Report as Assumption C, but equally essential to give value to the Report. The relations between this fourth assumption and the proposals and named assumptions of the Report will be discussed later under the heading: "A People's War for a People's Peace."

What is the meaning of Assumption C, that employment is maintained? The meaning is not that employment is made so continuous for everybody that there is never any unemployment at all. The social insurance scheme proposed in my Report includes as one of its important features insurance against unemployment: this assumes continuance of a certain amount of unemployment, during which income adequate for subsistence must be provided as of right, in the form of unemployment benefit. It assumes, in other words, that in any living, changing, and growing economic organization there will be occasions when individuals cannot be employed productively.

There will be intervals during which men whose previous work has ended will be standing by for new work, or during which labour will be idle because the raw material required or some other necessary factor in production has not arrived in time. There will be stoppages in the flow of work through weather, at home or abroad. There will be growth of demand for men at one factory or in one place, accompanied by decline in some other place. There will be seasonal variations in the demand for labour in particular industries. There will be unemployment due to technical changes in mechanical equipment or methods of organization, making unnecessary the work which particular men have done before and involving their transfer, perhaps after a training period, to new occupations. All these are forms of unemployment consistent with general prosperity and progress. They involve, as a rule, only short interruptions of earning and can be met fully by cash benefit. Provision must be made for them and can be made best by unemployment insurance.

In assuming that some unemployment will continue after the war and must be met by unemployment insurance, it is necessary also to make an assumption as to the rate of unemployment, that is to say as to what proportion of the persons insured against unemployment may be expected on an average to be unemployed at any time. The contributions required to meet the cost of unemployment benefit depend on the rate of unemployment as well as on the rate of benefit. The assumption made for this purpose in framing the financial basis of the social insurance scheme in my Report is of a future rate of unemployment of 10 per cent in the industries now subject to the general scheme of unemployment insurance. Over the whole body of persons who will be insured against unemployment, including those now exempted from insurance on the ground of the regularity of their work and those dealt with by special schemes, this means a rate of 8½ per cent: it means an average of 1½ million persons being unemployed at any one time and involves expenditure on unemployment benefit of about £110,000,000 a year. The social security scheme on its financial side is very far from assuming the abolition of all unemployment.

To many people the making of provision for unemployment on this scale will appear to be unduly pessimistic, implying acquiescence in an evil which could and should be cured. The answer to this criticism is that to make financial provision in an insurance scheme for the possibility of unemployment on a particular scale is not to admit that unemployment on such a scale is either necessary or tolerable. An unemployment rate of 10 per cent in the industries now covered by the general scheme of unemployment insurance is much higher than is involved in the various forms of unemployment described above as consistent with general prosperity and progress; in the prosperous south of Britain before the present war unemployment was running at 6 per cent or less. A rate of 10 per cent allows for substantial failure, either in controlling the trade cycle so as to prevent prolonged general depressions of trade, or in readjusting British industry to changed conditions after the war. In framing the financial basis of the security scheme, it is necessary to provide for the possibility of such failure; sound finance is cautious finance. This does not mean acquiescing in such failure or taking no steps to prevent it.

In relation to another of the risks covered by the social insurance scheme, that of sickness, the Government Actuary has allowed for the possibility that the more generous benefits proposed will increase materially—by one-eighth—the number of sickness claims made, in proportion to the number of persons insured. As a measure of caution in the financing of the insurance scheme, he has allowed for this happening, in spite of the great extension of the health services assumed in the Report. This does not imply acquiescence in the continuance of disease on its present scale or relaxation of efforts to prevent it.

To people of another school of thought, to allow for not more than 10 per cent of unemployment in the present insured industries may appear unduly optimistic. Recalling what happened after the last war, they look forward to a repetition of the same experience in the aftermath of the present war. That, it is suggested, is needless defeatism. In the last years before the war the finance of the general scheme of unemployment insurance was based on an unemployment rate of 15 per cent.; the actual unemployment in each of those years was much less than 15 per cent, though it included all the men whom years of neglect, in the depressed areas and contracted staple industries, had accustomed to idleness. There is nothing rose-coloured in the view that unemployment after this war can be kept down to a rate of 10 per cent, as compared with 15 per cent assumed as the average before the war. Unemployment in the war today is not 15 per cent or 10 per cent, but about $\frac{1}{2}$ per cent. Why should it be supposed that we have learned nothing from the experience of the last peace and must go back helplessly to 15 per per cent or 20 per cent or more?

For the purpose of an actuarial report on the finance of social insurance it is necessary to assume some particular rate of unemployment in future. But the social insurance scheme does not stand or fall by the accuracy of this actuarial estimate. If in practice the rate of unemployment can be kept below 10 per cent, as it is reasonable to hope that it can, there will be a surplus in the Social Insurance Fund available for other purposes. If the rate rises above 10 per cent—even materially above it—additional expenditure on unemployment may be more than covered by savings elsewhere, and could in any case be met by a relatively small increase of contributions.

Assumption C is not actuarial at all, but practical and human. It is not a prophecy that unemployment will be 10 per cent or any other rate. It is an assertion of policy:

that with provision of benefit for unemployment must go steps for the avoidance of mass unemployment, that is, avoidance of the permanent or prolonged involuntary idleness of large numbers of men, such as occurred during the last peace in the depressed areas of Britain or in Britain as a whole during the Great Depression of 1931 and 1932. On what reason or reasons is this assertion of policy based?

Five distinct reasons are given in paragraph 440 of my Report—five reasons for holding that avoidance of mass unemployment is one of the conditions of a satisfactory social insurance scheme.

Of five reasons set out in my Report, only the two most important need mention here. One reason is that payment of unconditional cash benefits is satisfactory provision only for short periods of unemployment; after that, idleness even on an income demoralizes. The other is that income security, which is all that can be given by social insurance, is so inadequate a provision for human happiness that to put it forward by itself as a sole or principal measure of reconstruction hardly seems worth doing. It should be accompanied by an announced determination to use the powers of the State to whatever extent may prove necessary to ensure for all, not indeed absolute continuity of work, but a reasonable chance of productive employment.

To say, however, that maintenance of employment is necessary for satisfactory social insurance does not mean that, if employment cannot be maintained, no social insurance scheme or a different scheme from that proposed is needed. The proposals of the Report are proposals for distributing the total income of the community, great or small, so as to put first things first: the provision of a subsistence income at all times and for all sizes of family, before provision of comforts for anyone. If, through failure to maintain productive employment, the total income avail-

able for distribution fell below a certain level, it might
prove impossible to abolish want completely. But it would
still be desirable to meet first needs first: the smaller the
total income, the greater the need to distribute it fairly.
Doubt as to the possibility of avoiding mass unemployment
after the war would not be a reason for having no scheme
of social security. It would make such a scheme all the
more necessary. But ought we to admit such doubts?
Putting the question positively, is it reasonable to make
Assumption C—that mass unemployment can be avoided
after this war?

II.—THE ASSUMPTION OF VICTORY

One answer to the question is that it is as reasonable
to make this assumption as it is to make another assumption, unnamed in my Report on Social Insurance, but as
completely underlying all its proposals, namely, the
assumption that Britain and her Allies can and will defeat
Germany and her allies. To the three assumptions named
in the Report for satisfactory social security after the war
has ended—(A) children's allowances; (B) comprehensive
health service; (C) maintenance of employment—a fourth,
Assumption D, must be added: that the war ends in
victory for Britain and her Allies. On any other assumption, planning for social security is not worth while.
Between Assumption D, that we can conquer Germany
in the war, and Assumption C, that we can conquer mass
unemployment after the war, there is, in fact, much
common ground.

First, each of these two assumptions, whether reasonable
or not, is necessary. If the war is lost, all it lost. If after the
war mass unemployment returns, the stability of British
institutions may be in peril. Vital political freedoms may
be sacrificed by a despairing democracy in the hope of
economic security.

Second, each of those two assumptions is about equally reasonable. The war, though swinging now in our favour, is not won; the forces of evil that have to be overcome are still terrific and unbroken. If Britain and her Allies can show the strength and unity and organizing power that will be required to crush the mechanized barbarism which two years ago seemed about to subdue the world, it is fantastic to believe that they are bound then to be defeated by unemployment.

Third, the general problems of realizing Assumption C and Assumption D are the same. To defeat Germany and her Allies it is necessary to organize to its utmost the production of Britain and her Allies, that is to say to plan and direct the use of all their resources in meeting the needs of war, in order of urgency and with the smallest possible waste of power. Maintaining productive employment after the war presents the same problem of using resources without waste in meeting the needs of peace. Though the needs of peace may appear less urgent than those of war, they are as great, and the general conditions for the solution of the two problems are the same: planning of the use of all resources by a single authority; fluidity of labour and other resources; international co-operation; determination to find a solution at all costs.

This does not mean that the problems of war and of peace are identical. War is temporary, while peace should be planned to endure; men will more readily surrender their sectional interests and compromise their political views in the passing exigiencies of war than they will accept what may appear to be a lasting sacrifice of cherished rights in peace. In planning for peace, moreover, it is essential to leave freedom for experiment, initiative, individual trial and error, without which progress cannot be assured. While the problems of organizing production in war and in peace respectively may be posed in the same general terms, the practical issues are different. Above all there is the political issue of the respective spheres of the State and of the individual, of central planning and of private enterprise.

This is the heart of the problem. On the subjects falling directly within the scope of my Report on Social Insurance there is or need be no cleavage of parties. Social insurance in Britain is not the property of any party and its development has long ceased to be a party issue. Social insurance is recognized as leading neither to one party camp nor to another. Proposals in this field can be judged on their own merits. Assumption C—maintenance of employment after the war—is in a different case. It is at once more important, more difficult and more urgent, than any other problem of reconstruction on the home front. It is more important, for it is the foundation of successful treatment of every other problem. It is more difficult, without any agreed solution between parties in this country and involving at the critical point of international trade co-operation with other countries. It is more urgent, because, if employment is to be maintained in the critical aftermath of war, the plans for doing this must be made now, and not when the war has ended. Is it possible that any plan for the maintaining of productive employment and avoidance of mass unemployment after the war can be made and agreed on now, can be made without disturbing national unity in the prosecution of the war itself?

That is not a question to be answered lightly. It cannot be answered finally, except practically, by the framing of concrete proposals which, when they are framed, find acceptance. My own view is that the search for such proposals is not hopeless, and that for two reasons. It is not hopeless, because the end is almost universally and passionately desired, so that any sacrifices that can be shown to be necessary and sufficient to obtain it will probably be made. It is not hopeless, because the road to maintenance of employment after the war probably is

not the road on which any of the main political parties
in Britain have travelled hitherto. We cannot trust to
private enterprise at private risk, which failed so badly
in the last peace. We cannot trust to any single panacea,
such as nationalization of all industries; mere change of
ownership and motive leaves the problems of organization
untouched.

We need a selective combination of methods; we need
various types of general control—of prices, of investment,
of transport and raw materials; we need probably public
monopoly ownership in certain fields, private enterprise
subject to public control in other fields, private enterprise
free of any save the general controls in yet other fields.
For the complex problem of maintaining employment in
the aftermath of war there is no simple solution that can
be made into a party cry. There is thus the possibility at
least of getting it treated as a technical problem rather than
a political issue—a problem as technical and as important
as the use of the different arms of war in the planning of
a military campaign. To discover whether the campaign
of peace, for giving ordered opportunity of service and
earning to all, can be treated in this way and conducted by
agreement to success, is one of the principal tasks of
national and international statesmanship today.

III.—A People's War for a People's Peace

One of the discoveries of the year 1942 is the deep and
vivid interest of the people of Britain in the kind of
Britain which is to emerge when the floods of war subside.
This interest in post-war problems implies no slackening
of war effort; it has been shown most conspicuously
in a year of war effort growing steadily and without
weariness to a climax. It implies no unwillingness to make
all the sacrifices required for victory. It represents simply
a refusal to take victory in war as an end in itself; it must

be read as a determination to understand and to approve the end beyond victory for which sacrifices are being required and the purposes for which victory will be used.

For the leaders of a nation at war, dealing as they must day by day with the urgent problems of each day, feeling directly the weight of the enemy's resistance and seeking to anticipate his thrusts, it is easy to feel that victory itself may be an end; that when at last they are in a position to impose their wills on the leaders of the foe their task will be done; that the performance of that task should not be complicated by consideration of what may follow its achievement.

It is possible that the common people of totalitarian countries, drilled from youth to be instruments of a tyrant's dream or a madman's revenge, living in the servitude of war for years before open war begins, may be incurious or fatalistic about their futures. For them victory or mere escape from war may seem an end. The common people of a pacific democracy are in different case. It will not appear to them sufficient reason, either for risking death in youth or for killing others, that they may thereby be in a position to impose their wills upon another people. They will fight to the death—all people will fight—in defence of their invaded homes. They can be roused for a time to anger against inhumanity abroad—as the British have been roused time and again, as the American people were in the first World War. But this anger may not last long enough to accomplish its aim. The sustained free effort required of the democracies today, to lead them to die and to kill in every quarter of the globe, until the forces of barbarism in every quarter are overcome, must be directed not by anger or fear or hate, but towards a clearly seen aim beyond the war—to the making of a world in which the common people of all nations and their children after them may live and work in security.

The people of a democracy, no less than those of a

totalitarian State, must have leaders. The difference between democracies and totalitarian States lies, not in absence of leaders, but in the power of a democracy to change its leaders without shooting. To have the power of peaceful change of Governments is the essential condition of a democracy. To exercise that power and make changes repeatedly or frivolously brings weakness in peace as in war. But desire for change can be prevented only by mutual understanding and trust between leaders and people. That is the real meaning of national unity in war.

National unity is not an affair of party bargains or coalitions. It can spring only from mutual understanding between Government and people. A vital factor in that mutual understanding today is recognition by those who govern of what has been described above as one of the discoveries of 1942, namely, the determination of the British democracy to look beyond victory to the uses of victory. This recognition in turn will be made easier by realization of the difference in the personal impact of war upon the common people and on those concerned with the daily tasks of government.

The most general effect of war is to make the common people more important. In war, needs become manifestly greater than the resources of man-power, machines, and materials available for meeting them, so that any waste of resources is a crime. Every able-bodied person in the community becomes an asset; all men can have the happiness of effort and of service; unemployment with its privations and frustrations disappears. All this happens because the urgency of the needs of war is recognized by the leaders as well as by the people, and by general consent the whole power of the State is used to organize resources so as to meet them.

Yet the needs of war, though they may be more urgent, are not in fact greater than the needs of peace. The needs of peace are as limitless as those of war. If and when a community reaches the stage when physical want has been abolished; if and when, proceeding beyond that point, it is able to ensure for all, on condition of service, comforts and material luxuries, as well as necessities, the limit of needs will not have been reached; new needs will arise and should be fostered by education—desires for leisure, for learning, for travel. But these stages are not in sight.

The condition of all peoples today leaves many needs unsatisfied which to those who feel them are as urgent as the needs of war. There is here another difference that requires to be overcome between the governors and the governed. Those in charge of affairs may find it easier to appreciate the urgency of the needs of war than that of the needs of peace, because for themselves the most urgent needs of peace have long been met. They may not always find it so easy from their own experience to realize the compelling necessity, in peace as in war, to organize resources for meeting needs, without waste or idleness. They are often engaged during war in much the same activities as those of peace, as Ministers, in Parliament, in the organization of parties or trade associations, in the higher administration of public affairs or of business. The coming of war does not mean for them what it does to millions of the common people, a violent change of occupations, with prospect of another violent change to an uncertain future when war ends.

This feature of war, as a time of violent changes in the direction of human effort and so of human occupations, involves change in the scope and functions of government. Automatic adjustment of economic activities by the price mechanism is too slow for times of rapid change; adjustment must be made directly by use of the powers of the State; adjustment will be made more rapidly and more smoothly in proportion as all the necessary measures have been planned beforehand. This is generally recognized of the changes required on passage from peace to war; it is as true, though not equally recognized, of the changes required in passing back again to peace.

It is axiomatic technically that preparations for war ought to be made before war begins, during peace; the fact that adequate preparations for war have seldom if ever

"SIR. THE STEED AWAITS!"

Reproduced by permission of the Proprietors of the "Evening Standard"

been made by modern democracies is due to a political obstacle—to their essentially pacific nature. It is as axiomatic technically that for smooth transition from war to peace adequate preparations must also be made in advance, that is to say planning for peace ought to be undertaken in war. Here there is no political obstacle. Planning ahead for peace even during war accords with the sentiment of democracies. It is one of the services desired by them of their leaders.

The more fully this fact is recognized, in principle and in the practice of government, the greater will be the unity of the nation in war, and the greater by consequence will be its strength for war. Only through complete mutual understanding between leaders and people can come the unswerving support and untiring effort for which the crisis calls. For the leaders of a democracy at war to concern themselves with the purpose of victory as well as with the means to victory is not a diversion of effort from more important to less important tasks. It is a part of their task—the means to success. Victory against an enemy as strong and as well prepared as our present enemy depends on making the war a people's war. One cannot make a people's war except for a people's peace.

IV.—THE NEED TO REMAIN UNITED NATIONS

This war is a war of Allies against a concentrated tyranny and its dupes and accomplices. Winning the war depends upon the Allies pulling hard and equally together until fighting ends in the surrender of the enemy. Winning the peace, that is to say, garnering the results of the victory, depends upon the Allies continuing to pull together and in the same direction after the fighting is over. If to win the war it is necessary to make the war a people's war, that means not the war of one people but of all the Allied peoples; it means that all the United Nations and not some only must even now be thinking of the uses of victory and must think the same things.

This does not mean that in all their economic and social legislation these nations must act together or do the same things. There are some fields of great importance to the people, in which each country may well take its own line because what it does cannot affect other countries. One of these is social security—the subject of my Report on Social Insurance. Social security as there described is income security. All my proposals are concerned simply with the re-distribution as between the citizens of Britain of the total national income so as to meet the most urgent needs before less urgent needs. If this Report, or anything like it, is accepted by Parliament, that will not mean Britain trying to make itself more comfortable than other nations or at the expense of other nations, or trying to get an undue share of the total wealth of the world. The plan of the Report is a plan for distributing whatever income we have in this country, whether small or large, in a certain way so as to meet the most urgent needs first.

Moreover, though many of the problems of social security are common to different countries, since all, or nearly all, countries are subject to unemployment, to sickness and industrial accidents, and to the ageing of their citizens, the methods to be adopted for dealing with these problems need not be the same in different countries. Differences in economic or political structure, in the degree of industrialization or density of population, in the development of voluntary insurance and in many other respects may call for varieties of method in dealing with the same problems of social security. The social insurance schemes of the three principal Allies—of the United States, of Russia, of Britain—are in fact very different from one another. They can continue to be different to suit the different circumstances of the three countries.

It is easy to think of other problems of reconstruction which, though of great importance, are also purely national in character. Dealing with the evil named in my Report as the giant Squalor is one of these. The methods to be adopted for securing the best possible distribution of industries and population, of good housing and healthy living conditions for all, need not be the same in different countries. Each nation can proceed on its own lines, learning, if it is wise, by the experience of other countries as well as by its own mistakes, but neither slavishly copying

H

nor delaying action itself for fear of how that action may affect its friends abroad.

But when we pass from such questions as social security or town planning and housing to the maintenance of employment, the position is changed. No one nation can wisely attempt to make a plan for giving to its citizens, not merely assurance of a minimum income, but what they need and desire much more—reasonable security of productive employment—without regard to the policies and circumstances of other nations. Every such plan must take account of the extent and the nature of international trade after the war and of the conditions, of equality or preference or special arrangements and controls, under which it should be conducted. Every such plan raises large issues of policy in the government of colonial dependencies.

More than that: if we are really to make a better world after this war, each nation must learn to recognize the truth that each gains by the prosperity of others, that if a nation in difficulties takes measures to relieve those difficulties without regard to their effect upon other countries, those measures may be defeated and may add to the difficulties of all. It is not possible to plan for security of productive employment and rising standards of life after the war except on the assumption of international collaboration after the war, in a world freed from the fear of renewal of war. To translate the generalities of the Atlantic Charter into practical terms is one of the most urgent tasks of statesmanship today.

The present war is not the first in which the people of this island have been engaged as partners in a widespread equal alliance against an enemy substantially single. In writing of the life and times of his great ancestor Marlborough, the present Prime Minister of Britain has described one of these earlier Grand Alliances, with its successes, difficulties, and failures; in many pregnant passages he has used the experience of that time to illumine the problems of succeeding generations, of today and of tomorrow. One of the most striking of these passages relates to the mood of "insensate economy" which disarmed England after the Peace of Ryswick in 1697.

"This phase," writes Mr. Churchill, "has often recurred in our history. In fact, it has been an invariable rule that England so steadfast in war, so indomitable in peril, should at the moment when the dire pressures are relaxed and victory has been won cast away its fruits. Having made every sacrifice, having performed prodigies of strength and valour, our countrymen under every franchise or party have always fallen upon the ground in weakness and futility when a very little more perseverance would have made them supreme, or at least secure. Now after Ryswick, as at Utrecht, as at Paris in 1763, as after the Napoleonic wars and Waterloo, and as after Armageddon, the island mainspring of the life and peace of Europe broke."*

There were, of course, defaults and weaknesses in other partners of the Grand Alliance then, as well as in England. But it is a simple matter of history that, within the period covered by this great biography, the Grand Alliance—first under William III and again under Anne—twice lost in peace much that it had won of security in war, and did so in large part because England as a principal partner twice pulled out of the team too soon, became isolationist, tried to go back to the past instead of building the future.

The problems and difficulties of alliances are not new and the lessons of the past apply to the full today. If the United Nations are to achieve victory without excessive sacrifice, they must act as one in the war. If they are not to risk throwing away after victory all or most of all of that for which they are sacrificing today their material

* *Marlborough*, vol. i, p. 489.

treasure and the lives of their young, they must continue united not only till fighting ends but thereafter. And just as national unity depends not on party bargains but on consciousness of a common aim, so international unity depends on the same consciousness and not on treaties or charters signed by leaders.

The United Nations have, in fact, a common cause and a common aim after victory as up to victory; they have the aim of treating victory not as an end but as a means to establishing justice among nations and security for service among citizens. The United Nations are in reality united by belief that "the object of government in peace and in war is not the glory of rulers or of races but the happiness of the common man."* The greatest danger against which, one and all, they need now to be on guard is that of forgetting, either in the wearied exultation of victory or in premature strife of parties, the reality which unites them for peace as much as for war.

* *Report on Socia Insurance and Allied Services*, para. 459.

11

FINANCE OF THE BEVERIDGE REPORT*

QUESTIONS

By SPENCER SUMMERS, M.P.

SIR WILLIAM BEVERIDGE describes his proposals as an attack upon the "Giant of Want." Such a challenge must command universal support. It can hardly be denied, however, that the plan goes much further than that, for many people are to receive benefits to which, if want is to be the criterion, they have no claim. It is true that they are to contribute to the benefits—other than children's allowances—but only to the extent of a quarter of the cost.

This position is brought about by the promise to pay benefits at subsistence level without any test of need. The case for fixing the rates of benefit at "subsistence" level for those "in want" is incontestable, but whether it is right, largely at the expense of the taxpayer, to provide benefits at subsistence level to people whose income already exceeds that level is surely an important question which ought to be examined. There is a natural and widespread dislike of any test of need, but there are many who see no justification for a compulsory levy on their resources to provide help for those who do not need it.

If the objective is to be the elimination of want, a test of need seems indispensable, and subsistence rates to those requiring them are logical. If, however, the abolition of a test of need is the object, then the whole subject must be looked at differently.

There is little doubt that a test of need tends to penalize

* *Observer*, 18th February, 1943; *Daily Herald*, 15th February, 1943.

thrift. That, in itself, is a good enough reason to consider whether it can be abolished, but it is clear that to do so will entail payments on a much bigger scale than would be required for the mere abolition of want and correspondingly increased contributions from all three parties to the scheme.

When the scheme is introduced, the additional cost to the taxpayer is £86 millions, or slightly below the cost of the scheme of children's allowances recommended. As time goes on, both the share and the amount paid by the taxpayer increases considerably, owing mainly to the rising scale of pension benefits, until, in 1965, the additional cost amounts to £254 millions, and the total cost to the taxpayer to £519 millions.

The question is frequently asked, "Can we afford it?" An attempt has been made to answer it by asking another— "Can we afford to do without it?"—but a constructive answer must be found which carries conviction. All those who have been injured in the war, the dependents of those who have been killed, and the millions of holders of Savings Certificates, have a right to feel confident that fresh commitments will not jeopardize their legitimate claims.

It is surely a sign of progress that such questions are viewed now with greater emphasis on the human, as compared to the purely economic, standpoint than they were twenty-five years ago, but we must guard against the danger of allowing emotion to replace judgment.

The word "afford" prompts people to think of their bank balance or their trouser-pocket, yet the apparently limitless resources of the Government during war tempts people to suggest that the analogy between the individual and the nation is misleading. This is not the place to examine the merits of that analogy, but the point can equally well be brought out by approaching it from another angle.

The contribution of the State is only another way of describing the contribution of the taxpayer. There must be some limit to his willingness to pay in peace-time, as well as a point beyond which it is harmful to go. Many would agree that the level to which taxation can be raised without detriment to the national interest is above that which existed before the war. At the same time, can it really be expected that the present taxation can be maintained indefinitely in peace-time? Where then is the right level; and will the proceeds of taxation at that level provide the initial £86 millions, and the additional sums required later for the Beveridge Plan, after meeting prior commitments?

The extent of our prior commitments will depend upon how long the war lasts and a number of questions which have still to be settled, but certain indications of their magnitude can be given. The interest payable on the National Debt increased last year by £70 millions. If that rate is maintained, by March 1944, it will have reached an annual charge of £250 millions more than the pre-war figure. War pensions cost £100 millions a year after the last war, and this seems as good a guide as any other to the cost after this war. The post-war cost of National Defence must be greater than it was and an increase of £150 millions might be taken as a provisional figure. We have already added £50 millions a year to the cost of Social Services since the war began. These four items alone come to £550 millions. We shall have obligations to stricken Europe; housing and educational development cannot be ignored; and further sums may be needed to keep down the cost of living. Taking these and all other factors into account it would seem not unreasonable to expect post-war budgets to be of the order of £1,600 millions or an increase of £700 millions over pre-war.

We raised as revenue in the last pre-war year from Income Tax and Surtax about £400 millions; from Cus-

toms and Excise, £340 millions; and from other taxation
about £160 millions: a total of about £900 millions.

Estimates of current revenue include £425 millions
from N.D.C. and E.P.T., but these burdens were imposed
as special war taxes. Income Tax and Surtax bring in
£600 millions more than they did pre-war, Customs and
Excise £460 millions more, while other taxation is about
the same. Such a marked increase in the revenue from
Income Tax and Surtax has only been possible by lowering
the income limit below which exemption is granted. Last
year those having incomes below £250 a year paid £100
millions more than they did before the war, and those with
incomes between £250 and £500 paid about £150 millions
more. It will be seen that nearly half the additional revenue
from Income Tax and Surtax together has come from the
smaller income taxpayers. It must be remembered, too,
that something like half of the increased revenue from the
smaller income taxpayers will return to them in the form
of post-war credits, and must therefore be regarded as
non-recurring.

Sir William Beveridge has shown that weekly sums in
excess of the compulsory contribution (4/3) are now
being paid for benefits to be included in the scheme.
If this be true there would seem to be no good reason why
taxation on the smaller incomes should be reduced to
compensate for the increased contributions to State Insurance which all will be required to pay. Nevertheless, it
is quite possible that a strong public demand will arise for
relief from direct taxation on the smaller incomes. If that
should occur it is to be hoped that those who are likely to
gain most from the Beveridge proposals will take into
account the effect that such relief might have on the
stability of the scheme.

The broad conclusion to be drawn from the above
figures is that about 65 per cent of the increased taxation
imposed during the war—apart from N.D.C. and E.P.T.—

may be required to meet our prior obligations after the war. To meet the Beveridge Plan a further 10 per cent would be required, leaving scope for relief from taxation of only about 25 per cent of the war-time burden.

Whether relief on this small scale would be sufficient to enable a high level of employment in peace-time and a real recovery of our export trade to be secured is a matter for experts to decide. In view of the uncertainty of the future, any forecast must necessarily be speculative, but this aspect of the matter must be studied.

These are some of the reasons why it is to be hoped that the implications of the Beveridge proposals will be examined realistically as well as sympathetically and without political or party bias. Such an examination might well include the question as to how far the proposals are really interdependent. If it were found that they could be introduced by stages we might in that way avoid having to retrace our steps at some later date. If Sir William himself can contribute towards a right judgment on these matters he will add to the debt which the nation already owes him.

ANSWERS

By Sir William Beveridge

Is it necessary for the abolition of want to provide for needs in all cases, irrespective of the other means possessed by the individual in need? This is the first question raised by Mr. Summers in his thoughtful paper. It is true that in order to be out of want as defined in my Report a man need not have more than a minimum subsistence income, and this could be secured in theory by a universal system of assistance subject to a means test in every case. But in practice such a system would not lead to abolition of want, because the citizens would in many cases suffer want rather than submit to investigation of their needs and means. I cannot believe that the British people would accept a scheme of universal assistance subject to a means test as giving them security or freedom from want. Nor can it seriously be maintained that money raised by a "compulsory levy" should not be used to provide benefits unless the beneficiaries can be shown by a means test to be without other resources; such an argument would exclude any State contribution to social insurance. Mr. Summers rightly recognizes the objection to a means test that it appears to discourage thrift, but hardly perhaps gives to this objection the importance that it deserves.

A larger proportion of the total savings of the community must clearly in future come from the moderate surpluses of many citizens rather than from the large surpluses of the few. But the essential condition for stimulating thrift to the utmost among all classes exposed to economic insecurity is to guarantee them benefits at need, irrespective of means and therefore not liable to be reduced when they are in need, as the result of their own personal thrift. To go as far as possible in dispensing with any means test is fundamental to my Plan. This does not mean that assistance subject to a means test can be abolished completely. There are abnormal and special cases which must be dealt with individually and in one substantial part of the field I contemplate the continuance for a time of assistance subject to means test, namely in the provision of assistance-pensions to those already of pensionable age or so near it that they cannot qualify for adequate contributory pensions under my proposals for a transition period. This exception from the general principle excluding means tests is a necessary piece of realism in the finance of the scheme, and is not open to serious objection as a discouragement of thrift. Those already of pensionable age are past the age of saving for pensions; men under forty-five are not affected by the transition period; of those within twenty years of pension age, the great bulk, by a very moderate saving of their own or small postponement of retirement, should be able to put themselves above the need of applying for assistance pensions.

"Can we afford it?" That is Mr. Summers' second question. Can the nation as a whole afford my Plan? That means, is the national income likely to be large enough, if fairly distributed, to give not less than the minimum for subsistence at all times for everybody. Just before this war, even with the mass unemployment which persisted after the dislocation of the previous war, there was within the wage-earning classes alone and without trenching on any of the profits or interests which were the main source of savings and investment, ample income, if wisely distributed, to keep every person well above want. To assume that we must be indefinitely much poorer after the war than we were before it is reasonless defeatism. The reasonable question is not whether we can afford this plan but when we can afford to begin it, and in what way the total burden can be most justly distributed.

Both of these are questions for serious examination. As to when we can afford the whole Security Plan, it is to be noted that for much the biggest item—that of retirement pensions—I propose incurring the full cost only at the end of a transition period. As to distribution of the burden, it can be argued that the contributions of insured persons should be increased, in relief of the taxpayer. As against this, serious arguments have been advanced that there should be no contributions at all by insured persons and that the whole cost of the scheme should be borne by taxation as in New Zealand. A compulsory insurance contribution can be described as a poll-tax, raised without reference to capacity to pay, and on that ground can be criticized as bad in principle. Though for reasons given in my Report I propose retention of the contributory principle, there is a limit to the contribution that can be exacted without hardship. The actual contribution that I propose will, I believe, be shouldered willingly by the great bulk of the insured persons, but it may be felt as a serious burden by those in receipt of low wages. Though in a table referred to by Mr. Summers,* I show that weekly sums in excess of the compulsory contributions are now being paid for security purposes, it must be remembered that this table gives averages paid by wage-earners of very different earning power. The table cannot be used to justify imposition of a compulsory contribution equal to this average and therefore much more than was being paid in many cases.

There remains the budgetary problem. It is right to dispel, as Mr. Summers does, the popular idea that when fighting stops and we turn from making means of destruction to make useful things we shall at once be able to afford almost anything. We are not paying for the war today either out of our own income or out of current income. There will be heavy burdens which can only be met by the Central Government in the immediate aftermath of war. For that reason my Plan proposes to keep the burden on the Exchequer low at the beginning and let it rise gradually as the total national income and the sources available for taxation increase. It is impossible to decide finally on the practicability of any actual figure without reference to data which are only in the possession of the Chancellor of the Exchequer and his officials. I can only say that I find it extremely difficult to believe that the sum of £86 millions, which is all the addition involved in my scheme to the budgetary costs of the first year, could not be found by suitable taxation.

At the end of his article Mr. Summers asks if my whole scheme is interdependent and invites me to suggest ways in which the total cost could be reduced or introduced gradually only. I should be churlish if I attempted no answer to this request. The initial £86 millions, as is

* *Report on Social Insurance and Allied Services*, paras. 285-6.

pointed out in the Report, could be cut down at once by
£10 millions if investigation showed that it was unnecessary
to put the large number of existing chronic cases of disability up to the new rates.

Another possible saving of about £23 millions indicated
in my Report would be to reduce the family allowances
by providing for the second child, when the father is
earning, not 8/– a week but 4/–. If the sole object of family
allowances were the abolition of want, then such a saving
might be worth consideration. But, in my view, it would
be wrong for two other reasons: as narrowing unduly the
gap between earning and benefit and because children's
allowances are wanted not merely for the abolition of
want but in order to improve both the quality and the
quantity of the population. There remains finally the suggestion that the cost of the Plan might be reduced by
making it less comprehensive. The difficulty is that the
only people whom it would seem justifiable to leave out
are those who, on the whole, even as insured contributors,
are likely to pay in more than they receive, the rich or
the "excepted" classes.

This relates to the burden on the Exchequer at the
outset of the scheme. The rate at which this burden will
grow depends in the main on the length of the transition
period for pensions, for which I have suggested twenty
years but which might in fact be lengthened or shortened
according to the rate of recovery from war-time dislocation. But it is necessary to face the political danger of
flexibility in this or other elements of the scheme; that is
to say, the danger of making the application of the scheme
the sport of party politics. I believe that the Plan, as I have
proposed it, is both just and feasible. If so, it would be in the
common interest for it to be accepted as an agreed settlement of the problem of want. If it is not so accepted, there
is danger that more will ultimately be spent under pressure
of discontent or sentiment or in political competition.

12

THE GOVERNMENT PROPOSALS AND THE BEVERIDGE REPORT*

1. A DIFFERENCE OF PRINCIPLE

THE nature of the debate in the† House of Commons upon the Report presented by myself to the Government at the end of November as to Social Insurance and Allied Services made it inevitable that, in its final stage, the debate should resolve itself into a discussion of how far the proposals of the Government accorded with those of my Report and how far they differed. This paper is devoted mainly to a study of the points of difference and an attempt to estimate their importance. A just preliminary to analysis of differences is to place on record the many important points on which the Government proposals agree with my Report. The points of agreement include introduction of children's allowances though on a lower scale, establishment of a comprehensive health service, unification of health and unemployment benefit and ending of the approved society system, grant of funeral benefit and making insurance comprehensive. All this within three months, even admitting the provisional character of the Government's conclusions, represents speed of action on a Report which can have had few parallels in peace. The nearest parallel known to me is in the announcement made by Mr. Winston Churchill in May, 1909, of the decision of the Government of that day to introduce a national system of Labour Exchanges, as recommended by the Royal Commission on the Poor Laws whose Report

* *Observer*, 24th February and 7th March. *Daily Herald* 1st and 8th March.
† See Note 9.

had been signed in February, 1909, and to combine with this a scheme of compulsory unemployment insurance.*

The Government proposals, as indicated by Sir John Anderson in the House of Commons, are based on my Report and accord largely with my Report. In considering how far these proposals differ from mine it is important to distinguish between differences of principle, procedure, and detail.

The main difference of principle lies in rejection by the Government of the fourth of the fundamental principles of my Report, namely, adequacy of benefit in amount and in time. In my Report it is stated that "the rates of benefit or pensions provided by Social Insurance should be such as to secure for all normal cases an income adequate for subsistence." In accordance with this, the rates suggested are based on a study of the cost of subsistence. On the assumption of a level of prices about 25 per cent above that of 1938, 40/– a week is proposed as the joint benefit or pension for man and wife together, and 8/– a week, in addition to an assumed 1/– a week in kind, is proposed as the average cash allowance for a dependent child. The full rate of pension, however, is to be paid not at once but only at the end of a transition period. For this, a length of twenty years is suggested. During those twenty years the actual rate of joint pension will rise gradually from 25/– to the full 40/–.

Sir John Anderson, on behalf of the Government, rejected the principle of relating rates of benefit to subsistence. He did this mainly on the ground that acceptance of the principle "would apparently imply the variation of benefits up and down with changes in the cost of living and a corresponding variation . . . in rates of contribution." He rejected the proposal for a rising scale of pensions in favour of "a definite rate of pension and a definite contribution, even if that initial rate is somewhat higher

* See Note 10.

than that recommended under the Beveridge scheme." No indication was given by any Government speaker of the "definite rate" of pensions contemplated. But, in view of the terms of Sir John Anderson's announcement and of the emphasis laid by the Chancellor of the Exchequer upon the necessity for avoiding heavy expenditure immediately after the war, it hardly seems possible that a rate higher, say, than 30/- a week in place of 40/- is contemplated for a joint pension. Such a rate would increase the cost of pensions at the outset of the scheme by something like £25 millions a year. It would increase the burden on the Exchequer by much more than that. The contributions proposed in my Report and in the memorandum of the Government Actuary for employers and insured persons are related to 40/-, not a 30/- joint pension, and would have to be reduced, leaving a larger initial deficiency to be met by the Exchequer.*

The ground for the Government's rejection of my pensions plan is apparently the fear of incurring excessive commitments for pensions. "Once contributions and benefits are fixed," said Sir John Anderson, "a very heavy commitment running into many hundreds if not thousands of millions of pounds would be immediately entered into." That, however, applies to the Government's own proposals as much as to mine. It is true that under my proposals the cost of insurance pensions rises from £126 millions in the first year of the scheme to £300 millions after twenty years; but only part of this is due to increase in the rate of pensions. Part is due to the increase in the numbers of people of pensionable age, while another part is due to

---

* As is pointed out in the following address on Social Security and Social Policy, taking into account both the higher initial rate of pensions and the lower contributions adjusted to a lower final rate of pensions, and assuming no other changes in the scheme, substitution of a fixed joint pension of 30/- a week for my proposed scale of pensions rising from 25/- to 40/- would increase the burden on the Exchequer in the first year by at least £50 millions.

bringing in for pensions persons now excluded; the acceptance by the Government of my principle of comprehensiveness means that at some time or other during the twenty years all the excluded classes must receive pensions at the Government's "definite rate" above my initial rate.

Without an actuarial study (for which I have no material) it is not possible to state precisely how much of the rising cost of pensions is due to these two factors, of increased proportion of old people and inclusion of new classes. It can, however, hardly be less than two-fifths the total increase of £174 millions; that is to say, only three-fifths of that increase is due to making the pensions rise from their original 25/– to their ultimate 40/–.*

If, moreover, as proposed by the Government, the original rate is more than 25/–, the difference between the cost in 1965 of their proposals and of my proposals is narrowed. The total cost of pensions, including assistance pensions, in 1965 on my plan is £325 millions. On the Government's proposals, assuming 30/– as joint pension, the cost can hardly be less than £265 millions. That is the difference between the pension commitment on my plan and on theirs—about £60 millions a year, twenty years after the end of the war.† That is less than 1 per cent of our national income today.

The difference of principle between the Government proposals and my Plan for Social Security comes to a head in their treatment of pensions. It is involved also in their proposals for children's allowances and for unemployment and disability benefit. At the assumed level of post-war prices the average subsistence cost per child, apart from rent, cannot be put below 9/–; the Govern-

* See Note 11.

† As is pointed out in the following paper only half of this £60 millions in 1965, would be a saving to the Exchequer: the rest would go to employers and insured persons through reduction of their contributions.

ment proposes 5/- in cash plus 2/6 in kind, or 7/6 altogether; this is a gap which must be filled somehow in
fixing scales of benefit, if these scales are to secure the
minimum for subsistence. In regard to unemployment and
disability benefit, the difference is not in rates but in
duration; the Government hold that each of these benefits
must be limited in time. This means that those whose
sickness continues after that time will be reduced to
pension level; those whose unemployment continues will
presumably receive unemployment assistance subject to a
means test. These proposals can be supported by administrative arguments. For the pensions proposal there is no
argument save financial.

It is not a valid objection to my principle of adequacy
of benefit that the cost of living may vary. My proposal
does not involve raising and lowering rates of benefit and
contribution with every change in prices. It does involve
fixing the money rates of benefit on a definite assumption
as to the future level of prices and having a Government
policy of keeping prices somewhere near that level. The
Chancellor of the Exchequer, in a recent Parliamentary
debate, indicated a policy or at least a hope of keeping to
a level of prices not very different from that assumed in
my Report. If that hope is realized, my rates can stand. If
headlong inflation takes charge, much more will be lost
than the Plan for Social Security.

Nor is it an objection to my principle that the present
chaotic variation of house-rents makes it impossible to
name any money rate of benefit or pension that will be
enough and no more than enough for subsistence in all
cases. That is a reason for dealing with the problem of rent
by replanning town and country and by adequate housing.
It is not a reason for abandoning any attempt to abolish
want.

The people of this country desire more than anything
else adequate provision for old age, an income of one's

own, without burdening one's children. There is no question of encouraging people to be old by paying them a larger than a smaller pension. There is the certainty, on the plan proposed by the Government, both of discouragement of saving because there will be a perpetual means test for pensions, and of a political auction between the parties to give adequate pensions. There is finally the fact that rejection of a rising scale of pensions means inevitably making the initial rate materially higher than that which I propose.

There is nothing sacred either about the initial rate proposed by me or about the length of the transition period. But my proposals as they stand can be defended as free from hardship, in full accord with the contributory principle, and saving money when it is most important to save it. The Government proposal weakens the contributory principle and increases the burden on the Exchequer just when that burden should be lightest, in the immediate aftermath of war when expenditure on military security must be higher than it is later. If the Chancellor of the Exchequer's arguments in discouragement of any financial commitments for social security are valid, the money to pay these larger pensions now will be taken from money which might otherwise have gone to better children's allowances, to speedier development of the health services, to education or to housing.

On my Plan, from about 1965 onwards, everybody but a small and diminishing fraction of old people will have pensions at the same rate as unemployment and disability benefit—at a joint rate of 40/- a week for man and wife. On the Government plan pensions will be fixed at a lower rate—obviously not enough to live on without other resources or dependence on children.

My Plan is not simply a plan to develop social insurance: it is a plan to give freedom from want by securing to each citizen at all times, on condition of service and contribution, a minimum income sufficient for his subsistence needs and responsibilities. It interprets, as any modern democracy must interpret, freedom from want to mean, not a claim to be relieved by the State on proof of necessity and lack of other resources, but having, as of right, one's own income to keep one above the necessity for applying for relief. My Plan takes as its aim abolition of want. The Government in regard to pensions wholly, and in regard to children's allowances and to unemployment and disability benefit to a lesser extent, abandon that aim.

II. Priority for the National Minimum

In respect of adequacy of benefit and pension and of children's allowances, there is a difference of principle between my Plan and the Government's proposals. It is appropriate next to deal with three differences between the Government proposals and my Report which compared with this are of a minor order of importance, though substantial. They relate to workmen's compensation, to industrial assurance, and to the proposed Ministry of Social Security. The way will then be clear for considering what was perhaps the main cause of dispute between the Government and its critics in the recent debate; this is the question of the time at which a definite decision should be taken on the Plan and its financial commitments. While in one sense this question is only one of procedure, it raises broad issues of social policy.

On workmen's compensation, the Government expressed no definite view, but suspended judgment entirely. They have not yet accepted the principle of unifying under one authority and on a social insurance basis, provision for disability of all kinds—whether due to industrial accident or disease, or to other causes. I hope they may shortly feel able to do so. The case for changing radically the present system is decisive. The details of my proposals, particularly on the financial side, are open to argument and variation, but I believe that, substantially as they stand, they would secure the greatest common measure of agreement, a fair distribution of burdens and a strong encouragement for prevention of accidents.

Of my proposal to convert industrial assurance from a competitive business to a public service, Sir John Anderson said merely, that with the rest of the Report the Government already had enough on their plate; Mr. Morrison treated this as a rejection of my proposal. I hope that this also is not a final decision. The proposal is bracketed in the Report as not integral to my Plan, not through any doubt as to its desirability but because my Plan is concerned essentially with provision of a minimum by compulsory insurance and not so directly with voluntary insurance. The reasons for the proposal as set out briefly under Change 23 in the Report and in Appendix D are extremely strong; it is a proposal made alike in the interests of the insuring public and of useful employment and fair treatment for the staffs of the industrial life offices. Unless some stronger reason for rejecting it can be given by the Government than has been given hitherto, it will be impossible to allay suspicion that rejection represents surrender to a highly organized sectional interest.

The question of a Ministry of Social Security may be treated either as a question of administration of the scheme when in force or as one of procedure for getting it into force. In the Report, it was treated as the former. I suggested an immediate decision to establish such a Ministry as the best means of administering the scheme, but not necessarily a decision to establish it immediately, as an organ for doing the preparatory work. That might be undertaken by some special authority—a Minister, a group of Ministers, or a body of Commissioners—charged to prepare the necessary legislation. There are obvious advantages of continuity in entrusting the preparatory work to the Minister who will begin the administration itself, but those advantages are not decisive.

In the Parliamentary debates, in view of the non-committal attitude of the Government, the immediate appointment of a Minister of Social Security came to be

JUST TO SHOW THEY MEAN BUSINESS
Reproduced by permission of the Proprietors of the "Evening Standard"

demanded as a proof of serious intentions. If that proof can be given otherwise, the question of the precise form of the preparatory machine becomes less important. The best proof of serious intention would be an undertaking to submit the legislation required for the unification at least of all central services within a fixed period, say not more than six months.

There remains the question of procedure. In both

Houses of Parliament, the Government held firmly to the refusal to commit themselves definitely to any proposals whatever until they could judge better of the financial position. They argued that no time need be lost by this refusal because legislation is required and must be prepared. By the time that legislation was ready they would also be in a position to judge better the financial prospects and to balance demands for social security against demands for other purposes.

Administratively this is a reasonable argument. Assuming full and equal speed ahead in either case on the preparation of the scheme, the date of its final operation will be the same whether the final decision in its favour is taken now or, say, six months hence. But it may be questioned whether six or even twelve months hence, if the war is still at its height, the major financial issues will be much clearer than they are today.

On the other hand, the Government's procedure loses the great psychological effect that might have been produced on the people of this and other countries by full and courageous acceptance of a policy of freedom from want. It raises inevitably doubt whether preparations will in fact proceed as rapidly on a plan that is hypothetical as on one for which there is a commitment. It leads finally to the certainty of continuing controversy, to risk of danger to national unity and to apparent or real dissipation of energies required for prosecution of the war.

All this could be avoided and the whole issue settled out of hand by acceptance of the principle that, in allocation of resources, provision of a national minimum for subsistence has priority over all purposes other than national defence. That is a principle which, I suggest, the Government of Britain should now accept as a directive from the democracy of Britain. A second directive is that the Government should take all necessary steps for the maintenance of employment after the war, being prepared to use the powers of the State so far as necessary for that purpose, subject only to the preservation of a limited list of essential British liberties, such as worship, speech, association, choice of occupation, and personal spending. In these two directives I believe are set the main lines of our home front policy for the reconstruction period. Acceptance of the first directive would remove all difficulties in the way of full and final acceptance of the Plan for Social Security for abolition of want which is in my Report.

That we can in due course after this war re-establish in Britain a standard of production and living high enough to abolish want, if income is rightly distributed, is beyond rational doubt. It is no objection whatever to the Plan that it commits future generations to such a re-distribution of income, by rising expenditure on pensions. All legislation involves commitments of this character; the commitment under my scheme is not significantly more than under any practicable alternative.

That the Exchequer will be able to bear the initial expenditure under the Plan, if that has priority, is equally not open to reasonable doubt. The Plan is designed to keep the burden on the Exchequer as low as possible at the outset. In its proposal for a rising scale of pensions, it reconciles the principle of a national minimum with financial exigencies as no other proposal can.

This is no time for timid counsels or party manoeuvres. The first step is for the Government to take their courage and imagination in both hands and accept now the principle of a national minimum for subsistence by social insurance as embodied in the Report. The next requirement is that it should find a reasonable spirit among its critics of all parties. We in Britain are not alone in the world or in the war.

As I said a few days ago:—

"If we in Britain devote ourselves for the next six months to arguing with one another about social security, we shall give the wrong impression abroad that we are thinking more about peace than about war. If, on the other hand, we take reconstruction in our stride, as in this matter on which at heart we are agreed we could take it, we shall show strength and unity; we shall give encouragement to ourselves and to all our Allies to get on with the war—to get on with a people's war for a people's peace."*

To reach this end is worth an effort. The way to it lies in recognizing that we should use the nation's resources remaining after defence needs have been met to provide a national minimum standard of living. We must recognize at the same time that this priority cannot be claimed for anything more than the irreducible minimum and that the practical steps to achieve freedom from want must take account, as the Report does, of the special financial exigencies of the immediate aftermath of war.

* Speech at Caxton Hall, 3rd March, 1943, printed below as Paper 13.

13

SOCIAL SECURITY AND SOCIAL POLICY*

WHENEVER there is any discussion of that document called the Beveridge Report—and there is quite a lot of talk about it nowadays one way or other, and in one place or another—there is one remark that is almost sure to be made by somebody. That is the remark that Sir William Beveridge himself has said that his scheme is impracticable unless employment is maintained and mass-unemployment is avoided. The last place in which the Beveridge Report was under discussion was the House of Lords and Lord Bennett there made the remark I've quoted: "Sir William Beveridge had himself spoken of the impracticability of his plan if unemployment rose to a certain figure." That is a misunderstanding, though I am sure a quite genuine misunderstanding. The time has come, I think, for Sir William Beveridge himself to say that he never said that.

I do use the word "impracticable" about one detailed provision of my scheme, in the event of mass unemployment: namely the proposal that when men had been unemployed for six months, if they still remained unemployed, they should be required to attend at a work or training centre as a condition of getting unemployment benefit. That proposal is easy, if there are only a few thousand or tens of thousands such men: it becomes impracticable if, through mass unemployment, there are hundreds of thousands of such men. But giving up that particular detail of the scheme would not mean giving up the whole scheme. I myself have made suggestions for adjusting the scheme in respect of this detail, if the amount of prolonged unemployment is excessive.

* Addresses under the auspices of the Liberal Party at Caxton Hall, 3rd March, 1943.

PUT ON THE TROUSERS

What I said in general and not in detail was, not that *my* scheme is *impracticable*, if there is mass unemployment, but that *no* scheme of social insurance is *satisfactory* if there is mass unemployment. There is all the difference in the world between the two statements. The first suggests that if there is mass unemployment you might be better off with a different scheme than mine or with no scheme at all. The second statement means that to make a good job you want both things—both social insurance and prevention of mass unemployment. It is like saying that no man is satisfactorily dressed unless he has both coat and trousers; that does not mean that till he is sure of his coat he will be warmer without any trousers. In being asked to report on social insurance and allied services, I was not asked to say how employment should be maintained; I was not asked to design a complete suit—only the trousers. I have designed the trousers, that is to say, the scheme of social insurance. My advice is that we had better put the trousers on at once, so that with a free mind we can see about a coat as well (that is to say maintenance of employment) and about other parts of our reconstruction wardrobe (that is all the other things we have to do, in dealing with disease and bad housing conditions and insufficient education, to make the New Britain that we want).

Of course, trousers depend to some extent on what goes on other parts of the body. They need to be kept up—by braces. If you are not tired of the metaphor, you can compare the finance of the insurance scheme to the braces of the trousers: a pessimist is sometimes defined as a man who wears both braces and a belt. Now, it is true that at a certain point of growth of unemployment, it might become impossible to pay for the social insurance scheme. That would happen if all of us took a holiday for life;

unless most of us do a reasonable amount of work we cannot enjoy a reasonable standard of living. But, actually, my scheme in its finance allows for a very substantial amount of unemployment—for 10 per cent in the present insured trades—for a million and a half persons on an average always being unemployed. I do not believe that there is the slightest reason why we should have as much unemployment as that, or anything like it, if we organize our economic life properly. But as a measure of financial caution the Government Actuary and I agreed that we ought to allow for a substantial amount of unemployment in the social insurance scheme. The finance of the scheme is based on that assumption of a million and a half unemployed.

That seems to me plenty to allow for; but my allowing for it does not mean that the scheme must break down financially if there is more unemployment, if, instead of one-and-a-half millions, there were two millions or even two-and-a-half millions. The expenditure on unemployment is only a small proportion of the whole Social Security Budget—about one-eighth. Pensions alone cost three times as much as unemployment in the budget, to say nothing of the children's allowances, the medical service and sickness and accidents. If one found one had to pay more than one expected for unemployment, one might easily find that one was saving on the other side of the account more than enough to pay the excess. If one did not have compensating savings elsewhere, one would have to raise the contributions and there is nothing to prevent one from doing so. The finance of the Social Insurance Scheme is not rigid: it is elastic. The best trouser braces *are* elastic.

NOT A ONE-MAN REPORT

There is another remark often made about the Beveridge Report—I rather believe that Lord Bennett made this one also—and that is that the Report is a one-man Report. Now, it is true that the Report is signed by one man only—myself—so that I am the only person that can be hanged for it. No one else can be brought to book for anything whatever that is said in it. No one else is committed to it. But it is not true that the Report was made, or could have been made, by one man sitting and thinking and studying by himself. I had sitting with me a Committee representing all the Departments concerned with the problems under consideration—all the best experts in the Government service—and very good experts they are. They acted as a Committee in examining witnesses, in discussion and in criticism. They acted as my technical advisers. Without their help in all these ways the Report would have been a very different and much inferior document. I alone am responsible for all that it proposes, just as a Minister alone is responsible for everything that is done in his Department. I was like a temporary Minister for devising this particular piece of post-war reconstruction; I could not have done the job otherwise.

Real Ministers would not be able to do much without their Departments. It has often been noticed how different are the speeches which politicians make when they are Ministers, with all the knowledge and ability of their Departments behind them, and the speeches which they make in opposition when they have nothing to trust to but their own intelligence and knowledge. Those opposition speeches sometimes are very flimsy and dull by comparison with the wealth of knowledge, the grasp of the subject and even the humour that is displayed by Ministers sitting on top of their Departments. Though it is the same mouth out of which the speech comes on each occasion.

THE BRITISH PEOPLE BECOME ARTICULATE

There is another sense also in which my Report is not just what one man thought up by himself. In addition to having at our disposal all the expert knowledge in the Government Departments, we received memoranda from the experts outside the Government service—trade unions, employers, friendly societies, local authorities, insurance companies, organizations of political parties, organizations of women, organizations for social service, and many more; we learnt an immense amount from these witnesses. The principal memoranda of these outside organizations have been printed as a companion volume to my Report, and it is a volume well worth studying.* The main result of studying it is to show how much agreement there was, even before my Report was made, upon almost all its main principles.

The main feature of my Plan for Social Security is a unified comprehensive scheme of social insurance to be administered by one Department, to provide cash benefits adequate in amount and in time without a means test, at a flat rate of benefit in return for a flat rate of contributions. With this goes a comprehensive health service and a system of children's allowances. Having these features in mind, I suggest that some of you should read the memoranda submitted to my Committee by, say, the Association of Municipal Corporations, the Trades Union Congress, the Shipping Federation (which was the only employers' organization to make definite general recommendations) and the National Council of Women of Great Britain. All those bodies, generally interested in social insurance and not in one side of it only, and other bodies of general interest, such as Political and Economic Planning, put up proposals agreeing on practically all those

* *Social Insurance and Allied Services.* Memoranda from Organisations. Appendix G to Report by Sir William Beveridge, Cmd. 6405, 2/-.

main principles. Of course, there are differences both as between the different organizations, and between what they said and·my proposals. Since they differed among themselves, I could not agree with everything that all or any of them said. But if you will study what was said to my Committee by these outside organizations of general interest, such as I have named, you will see that my Report represents to a very large extent the greatest measure of common agreement in the views of those who have thought most seriously upon its problems. That is what I tried to make it. I tried to make a Beveridge Report which would really be the British people become articulate about what they want in the way of social security. I hope that to some extent I may have succeeded.

THE NATIONAL MINIMUM A BRITISH IDEA

My Report as a whole is intended to give effect to what I regard as a peculiarly British idea: the idea of a national minimum. My Plan for Social Security is part of a policy of a national minimum. The idea of a minimum wage, which we learnt from the trade unions and have embodied in Trade Boards Acts, is necessary but isn't sufficient. There is wanted also a minimum income for subsistence when wages fail for any reason; a minimum of provision for children; a minimum of health, of housing, of education. A minimum needn't be static; in every field it should progress. But being a minimum only it leaves room and incentive to individuals to add to it for themselves according to their personal capacities and desires. The national minimum—preserving the maximum of liberty and room for progress while putting an end to want and other evils—is a peculiarly British idea. My Report is intended to give effect to that idea in one important field—that of income.

But my Report is only a Report. It's not the law of the

land—only recommendations to the Government. What have the Government done about it? They've accepted a great deal of the Report—not the whole; and they've accepted it provisionally only, subject to final decision when they've looked more closely at the finance. Unfortunately one of the points which they haven't accepted is rather central to the whole. My proposals are part of a policy of a national minimum. In respect of pensions, and to a less extent in relation to the period of unemployment and disability benefit and the rate of children's allowances, the proposals of the Government, as outlined in the recent debate, depart from the principle of a national minimum. At the same time, they involve greater financial difficulties. Let me try to explain just how that happens.

FIXED AND RISING PENSIONS

For pensions I proposed the same basic rate as for unemployment and disability—40/- a week joint pension for man and wife—but that this basic rate should be paid only after a transition period of twenty years during which pensions would rise by scale from 25/- joint to the final 40/-; contributions would be throughout for the 40/- pension. The Government propose a fixed pension, even if it is "somewhat above" my initial rate. That's bound to be much more expensive to the Exchequer at the outset of the scheme. The Government haven't said what fixed rate of pension they contemplate. For the purpose of comparison, I'll assume 30/- a week joint; they can hardly give less and to give more from the beginning merely makes the cost all the greater. My plan means that every man contributes from the beginning for a full basic pension of 40/- and gets the full pension if he contributes for twenty years or more; if he's over 45 he contributes for a shorter time before reaching 65 and has a smaller but still, in most cases, very substantial pension; if he's so old that he has no chance of getting an adequate contributory pension, he can get exemption from contributions.

That very briefly is my plan. As compared with that, the Government plan means that everybody contributes not for 40/- but for a 30/- joint pension; no one ever gets more than 30/- however long he contributes. That's more expensive to the Exchequer at the outset in two ways—because the Exchequer has to find money for 30/- pensions to everybody in place of 25/- pensions and because the contributions from insured persons and their employers are lower. If the pension is fixed (say) at 30/- a week the burden on the Exchequer—through higher pensions and lower contributions from employers and insured persons—is at least £50 millions more than on my proposal in the first year and it stays more for many years. At the end of the transition period—twenty years later—my plan giving 40/- pensions costs only £60 millions more than a fixed pension of 30/- would cost, and only half of this addition falls on the Exchequer, that is to say on the tax-payer. The other half is provided by contributions of insured persons and their employers.

If the pension rate is fixed at any other point, the argument isn't affected. At 35/- the additional burden on the Exchequer would be even greater at the outset and the ultimate saving less; at say 28/- the additional burden at the outset would be only a little less than £50 millions, because the contributions from employers and insured persons would be still lower. With a fixed pension, whatever the rate, in place of a rising scale, a less satisfactory provision for security burdens the Exchequer most just at the wrong time, in the immediate aftermath of war. The relief twenty years after is not worth getting at the cost of sacrificing the national minimum of subsistence. How any Chancellor of the Exchequer can have been persuaded to contemplate such a scheme, passes my comprehension.

My proposal for a rising scale of pensions is the way,

and I believe it is the only way, of reconciling the principle of a national minimum with the exigencies of post-war finance and with the contributory principle. It is identical in principle with the pension plan of New Zealand, the only other country which aims at social security comparable to that of my plan. The proposals of the Govern-

"JUST WAIT A LITTLE, WHILE I MAKE SOME SLIGHT ALTERATIONS."
Reproduced by permission of the Proprietors of the "News Chronicle"

ment were stated as provisional. I hope they'll reconsider this one about inadequate fixed pensions, and also the inadequate children's allowances.

REALISTIC FINANCE

My plan faces up realistically to the financial difficulties of reconstruction. It stands firmly by the contributory principle, because it is insurance, not charity. Contributions for pensions, if they're to mean anything, must be paid over a long period: it isn't contributory to expect to get a pension of 40/- a week for perhaps twenty years of old age, by paying 2/- or 3/- a week for five years before then. Of course, my plan means that those already of pension age or so near it that they can't contribute for more than a few years can't qualify for adequate contributory pensions as of right. They'll be able to get adequate pensions if they need them—that's part of the scheme—but they'll have to show need.

There's nothing sacred about my suggested initial rate of 25/- a week joint pension. If the Exchequer could find the money to start pensions at 30/- or more in place of 25/-, provided they went by scale to 40/- automatically, I'd have no objection—on one condition: that this extra money at the outset mustn't be taken from more important things, like a proper medical service or adequate children's allowances. Even if there are to be a few lean years just after the war, we mustn't cut down on those. And I don't believe that my proposals, if they were adopted substantially as they stand, would involve any hardship on anybody, young or old.

Of course, in one sense, it's hard to have been born too soon to benefit fully by this Plan for Security. Each one of us is apt to find that he's been born at the wrong moment—particularly in times of revolution or war like this. But if the difficulties of the immediate aftermath of war are going to make it difficult to do for the older people just everything that we'd like to do, unless we're to sacrifice the future and the children, I believe that the older people themselves wouldn't ask for that sacrifice. After all, people of my age or near it, haven't been called on to give our lives in war as so many of the younger people have done. The younger people were born at the wrong time in another way.

NOT A PARTY QUESTION

The national minimum of subsistence is a British idea also in the sense of not being the property of any one political party in Britain. Practically all of us, I believe, accept it, and accept for it a priority in the allocation of national resources second only to military security. First things first: bread for all on condition of service before cake for anybody. We all accept that. There is the explanation of the reception given by the people to my Report and of the support by so many leaders of the Churches. With that priority it is obvious that we can afford a minimum above want, when real peace returns. The only problem is that of keeping down State expenditure in the immediate aftermath of war, when military costs will still be high and when State money will be needed for physical, economic and social reconstruction in many fields at home and abroad. My Plan recognizes and solves that problem. The Government, according to their spokesmen, think that they have accepted my Report in principle, subject only to a caution about finance. They haven't quite done so, but I believe that they'd like to accept it. If they will look at the finance of my scheme again, their doubts should vanish.

It would have been possible by a small change in the Government's attitude to settle this problem of want by acclamation, as the problem of women's suffrage was settled in the last war—because at heart we are agreed. Women's suffrage was settled by agreement in the last war, largely because the work that women did in the war brought home to everybody their equal capacity for all the duties of citizens. One effect of this war, as I wrote the other day, has been to make common people more important. But I'm not sure that that's the best way to put it. We are all common people; in this besieged and attacked fortress island, we have passed through the same experiences and have realized our common humanity as never before. The Nazi bombs and the measures that we had to take for safety against them allowed no distinction between rich and poor. My Plan for Social Security makes no distinction either. It is a plan for all citizens without distinction of rich and poor. Might it not come by agreement out of our war-time experience? I hoped—most people hoped—that this was going to happen. I hope and believe that this may still be possible. It will be possible, if the Government take their courage and imagination in both hands and accept my aim of abolishing want. There is plenty of courage and imagination in this Government —at the very top.

Taking Reconstruction in our Stride

It rests with the Government in the first instance, to move forward a little further and faster than they've moved up to now. But if that does happen and the Government feel able now to give to the national minimum of subsistence the priority which it should have in allocation of national resources, there'll be a call for equal reasonableness from those who have been dissatisfied with the Government hitherto. One can't claim priority for more than the minimum, and ask for benefit or pensions now above subsistence level. One mustn't ignore the difficulties of finance in the immediate aftermath of war; there'll be a time of special effort and sacrifice when we must be reconstructing our economic life, as there was for Russia in building up the capital structure of her industry. One mustn't play party politics or yield to any sectional interest, however vocal or highly organized; the times are too critical for that.

We British aren't alone in the world or in the war. If we in Britain devote ourselves for the next six months to arguing with one another about social security, we shall give the wrong impression abroad that we are thinking more about peace than about war. If, on the other hand, we take reconstruction in our stride, as in this matter on which we are agreed we could take it, we shall show strength and unity; we shall give encouragement to ourselves and to all our Allies to get on with the war—to get on with a people's war for a people's peace.

14

CHILDREN'S ALLOWANCES AND THE RACE*

MOST of those who have advocated children's allowances in Britain have done so mainly or wholly on economic grounds; they have stressed the importance of such allowances as a means of preventing want and improving the nurture of the rising generation. The recommendation of children's allowances in my recent Report on Social Insurance rests almost entirely on such grounds, for these alone fall directly within the scope of the Report. But children's allowances, that is to say, adjusting the income of adults in one way or another to their family responsibilities, must be considered from other aspects also. How would the giving of allowances for children affect the number of children born, that is to say, the quantity of the population? How would it influence the kind of children born, that is to say, the quality of the breed?

The first of these questions is referred to briefly in my Report. After pointing out that, with its present rate of reproduction, the British race cannot continue and that "means of reversing the recent course of the birth-rate must be found," the view is expressed that "it is not likely that allowances for children or any other economic incentives will, by themselves, provide that means and lead parents who do not desire children to rear children for gain." "But children's allowances can help to restore the birth-rate, both by making it possible for parents who desire more children to bring them into the world without damaging the chances of those already born and as a

* Memorandum prepared in connection with Galton Lecture, 16th February, 1943 (see Note 12).

signal of national interest in children, setting the tone of public opinion."*

The second question, as to effect on the quality of the children born, is not considered at all in my Report. But it cannot be left out of account in deciding on social policy. The first reaction of many people, when this question is raised, is to express the fear that children's allowances, however desirable on economic or social grounds, would be likely to lower the quality of the population, by stimulating the birth-rate solely or mainly among the poorest classes. One reply to this view is given by what has been said above in considering the effect of children's allowances on the number of births. Such allowances could not influence one way or another those who take no thought at all, the thriftless and the careless. It would increase families only where the parents desired children for their own sake but refrained from adding to their families for fear of injuring those already born, that is to say, parents with a high degree of social virtue, and likely to care well for their children.

PROFESSOR FISHER'S EUGENIC ARGUMENT

Another reply is found in the argument advanced by Professor R. A. Fisher, that children's allowances are a direct and necessary way of correcting the present dysgenic tendencies in our population and improving the quality of the race. This argument, set out by Professor Fisher in 1931 in a paper on "The Biological Effects of Family Allowances,"† in the light of his work *The Genetical Theory of Natural Selection*,‡ can be put shortly as follows:

The birth-rate in Britain today, as in most if not all other civilized countries for which data are available, is inverted, in the sense that it is higher among the less

---

* *Report on Social Insurance and Allied Services*, para. 413.
† Printed in the *Family Endowment Chronicle*, November, 1931.
‡ Published by Clarendon Press, Oxford, 1930.

prosperous and less successful classes of the community than among the more prosperous and more successful. Taking together all the learned professions and every grade of teachers and clerks, taking, like the census authorities, all occupations socially equal to or superior to that of a railway booking clerk, Professor Fisher calculates that their rate of reproduction is only half that of the general population, is only 40 per cent of the numbers needed to replace them. But inversion of the birth-rate is not confined to a difference between wealthy or highly-educated classes and other classes in the country or between professional men and women and wage-earners. It extends throughout the social scale, making artisans generally less prolific than their assistants, semi-skilled classes less prolific than the unskilled.

The accuracy with which economic rewards are related to abilities and services in modern societies is a matter on which there is room for legitimate difference of opinion. That there is some relation cannot be denied by any reasonable man; in each economic or social class ability to render service makes itself felt; the more able tend to obtain greater rewards than their colleagues and to secure for themselves or their children the better chance of promotion to work that is more highly valued. With an inverted birth-rate this means promotion to a class with a lower birth-rate. In Britain, as elsewhere throughout the civilized world, economic and biological influences are at cross-purposes. The position is summed up by Professor Fisher as follows: "Since the birth-rate is the predominant factor in human survival in society, success in the struggle for existence is, in societies with an inverted birth-rate, the inverse of success in human endeavour. The type of man selected, as the ancestor of future generations, is he whose probability is least of winning admiration or rewards for useful services to the society to which he belongs."*

* *The Genetical Theory of Natural Selection*, p. 227.

SOCIAL PROMOTION OF THE INFERTILE

What has caused the birth-rate in Britain to be inverted? The question may be put in another way by asking of the two sides of the phenomenon, which is cause and which is effect. Does economic success lead to the biological failure of infertility, or does biological failure lead to economic success? Most people offhand would give the former answer, and attribute the lower birth-rate of the more prosperous classes to their prosperity. The answer given by Professor Fisher is the direct contrary of this. He holds that "the differential birth-rate itself is entirely accounted for by the social promotion of the less reproductive compared to the more reproductive strains in the population; and that in the absence of this promotion, which continually lowers the fertility of the better-paid classes (whether this fertility is determined by physical or, what is more important, by mental or moral characteristics) the more prosperous classes would show the higher rate of reproduction."

The argument is that the economic structure of all or nearly all civilized communities today, in so far as it puts the whole or most of the burden of rearing the next generation on individual parents, puts a premium on infertility and, other things being equal, improves the chances of the solitary child as compared with the children of large families. In the poorer classes, to belong to a small family rather than to a large family means for the child better feeding, clothing and housing, less probability of actual want, less need to earn as soon as possible, and therefore more chance of higher education. In the wealthier classes it means greater prospect of preparing for expensive and well-rewarded professions and a larger inheritance. There are two distinct routes of social promotion, by ability and by infertility; as compared with the classes below it, each class has a large proportion of infertile strains. Since in any stratified society people marry mainly within the same social class, this means that those promoted by ability are more likely to make infertile marriages than if they had not been promoted. In every civilized society the meeting and mating of ability and infertility in the higher social classes tends to breed ability out of the race, and prepares the way for the decay of that society. The classic illustration of this process, given long ago by Galton, was the tendency of men who had risen to eminence by ability— as judges, commanders, statesmen—or the sons of such men, to marry heiresses for the support of the peerages that they had acquired: heiresses were predominantly drawn from infertile stocks and the "destroying influence of heiress blood" led shortly to the extinction of the peerages. A similar inversion of the birth-rate heralded the decay of the Empire and the civilization of Rome.

From this analysis of the inverted birth-rate and its cause, in the social promotion of infertile stocks, Professor Fisher deduces the eugenic argument for children's allowances: "Two entirely different lines of sociological enquiry have thus converged to concentrate attention upon a singular anomalous feature in our economic system— the great differences in standards of living between persons performing the same economic services, but having different family responsibilities. From the economic standpoint we may recognize this anomaly as *wasteful* . . . as *unjust* . . . and as *demoralizing*. . . . From the biological standpoint we may recognize that exactly the same social anomaly has the peculiarly pernicious effect of segregating the heritable factors which make for a low rate of reproduction and of uniting them with all such socially valuable qualities as enable the citizen successfully to play his part in social co-operation." Children's allowances, to the extent that they neutralize the economic advantage of belonging to a small rather than a large family, must have a directly eugenic effect of checking the selective social promotion of infertile stocks.

This is the eugenic argument for children's allowances as put forward by Professor Fisher. Two criticisms can be made on it.

Two Criticisms Examined

One criticism is that the positive side of Professor Fisher's thesis appears to be better established than the negative side. He maintains positively that the premium on small families in every class, leading to the social promotion of infertile strains, causes inversion of the birth-rate; he maintains negatively that there is no other cause of this inversion, that is to say, that prosperity, ability, education are not themselves a cause of the lower fertility that is found among those who possess them. The negative conclusion appears open to question. On the one hand it is hard to believe that there has been time for selection by itself to bring about the great differences observed between the different classes. On the other hand, it is certain that, during the past seventy years at least, fertility in Britain, as in all similarly situated communities, has been affected profoundly by birth control. It is hard to believe that the extent to which birth control is practised by persons of different social classes has not been influenced by differences in respect of wealth, standard of living, access to birth control information and so forth.

A second criticism is that the principal data as to inversion of the British birth-rate used by Professor Fisher are drawn from the census of 1911, and that the inversion may have become much less marked since then, through spread of the practice of birth control. Unfortunately, the question asked in the census of 1911 as to the number of children each person had had was not repeated in the same form in later censuses, so that this suggestion cannot easily be put to any final test. A recent American writer on this subject, Mr. Frederick Osborn, states that there are indications that, with the further spread of birth control which appears inevitable, social class differences in fertility will narrow and gives this as one of the reasons why he himself fails to view the eugenic aspects of differential fertility with alarm. Yet, on data for the United States coming down to 1935 or later, Mr. Osborn admits for the States, in terms much the same as those of Professor Fisher for Britain, that "whatever changes may occur in the future, for the present in this country persons at the lowest socio-economic level have the most children; there are fewer children per family with each increase in the socio-economic level, until we reach the highest income group, who may show an increase in children."*

How far do these criticisms affect Professor Fisher's eugenic argument for family allowances? The answer is that they affect it in form, rather than in practical conclusion. Indeed in some respects they strengthen the case for such allowances and for their extension in new forms. Even if the negative side of Professor Fisher's thesis—that there is no cause of differential class fertility other than the selection of infertile stocks for social promotion—is rejected, that does not affect the positive side of his thesis: that selective social promotion of the infertile must tend to breed inherited ability out of the race. And even if the differences between classes are narrowing through the spread of birth control, there is no evidence that they have narrowed to insignificance either in Britain or in America.

SUPPLEMENTATION OF SUBSISTENCE ALLOWANCES

There appears still, on the face of it, to be a strong eugenic argument for children's allowances to reinforce

* Frederick Osborn: *Preface to Eugenics*, pp. 133-4. (Harper, 1940.)

the economic argument. The eugenic argument, moreover, points to a development of such allowances far beyond the subsistence level that is sufficient for abolition of physical want.

A subsistence grant for each child equalizes conditions between the large and small family only in respect of families whose income is at or near subsistence level— that is to say, only in the lowest paid section of the community. From a larger income more is habitually and inevitably spent on the rearing of each child. Even with my proposed subsistence allowance, the economic advantage of belonging to a small rather than to a large family would remain for every section of the community above the poorest. Social promotion from all sections above the poorest, including all the better-paid wage-earners as well as the professions, would still be influenced by infertility, would still on Professor Fisher's argument lead to some destruction of the ability now in these classes.

The logic of Professor Fisher's argument involves complete equalization between the large and the small family for each income class. It involves the adoption of the principle described by him as that of equal standard of living for equal work, in place of equal pay for equal work, in every class of the community. It suggests that even without following this logic to its final conclusion of universal allowances for children, proportionate to the parents' income in every case, the subsistence allowance of my Report needs supplementation. Two practical ways of supplementation deserve serious consideration.

The first way is the development of occupational schemes of children's allowances, for professions such as the public service both central and local, teaching both in Universities and in schools of all kinds, medicine, law and accountancy. In these and in other occupations in which entry depends on ability and is substantially open to trained ability, regardless of family, there should be schemes of children's allowances on a scale much greater than the subsistence scale proposed in my Report and graded perhaps by the parent's income. The cost of these allowances should be met not out of general taxation, but either by the employers alone where there were employers as an addition to salary, or by joint contributions by employers and employees to a common pool, or by contributions from the prospective beneficiaries alone. In this way the existing premium on infertility would be removed or diminished just where it is most damaging today, among occupations selected for ability.

INCOME TAX REBATES

The second practical suggestion involves the maintenance, and, if necessary, the extension of the system of income tax rebates in respect of children. The idea sometimes mooted that grant of children's allowances on a subsistence scale, as proposed in my Report, should lead to abandonment of income tax rebates, is wrong and reactionary. Income tax in future is likely to cover a much larger proportion of the population than in the past, including many skilled wage-earners. Through provision of substantial rebates it affords an invaluable means of removing in all classes, not merely in the professions by occupational schemes and in the unskilled classes by subsistence allowances, the premium on infertility with its damaging effect on inherited ability. Intellectual ability, though commoner in classes that have been selected for it than in other classes, is not confined to any class and is widely distributed. All social classes, except perhaps the very lowest of all, have substantial proportions of children with more than the average of intellectual ability. And in all social classes, except perhaps the richest of all, the able member of a large family has less economic opportunity than if he belonged to a small family. The skilled wage-earners by their quality and their numbers represent probably the largest store of heritable ability in the country and a store which it is vital to keep as large as possible.

SOME OBJECTIONS ANSWERED

The argument for children's allowances on eugenic grounds, if not as easy of popular acceptance as the argument on economic grounds, cannot be dismissed. It supports the proposed general scheme of subsistence allowances irrespective of means. It points to the need for supplementing general children's allowances on a subsistence level, by occupational schemes and tax rebates on a higher level. It remains only to consider shortly some possible objections to endeavouring to use allowances for children in this way, as a means to improvement of the race.

First, there is nothing undemocratic in such a proposal. The differential birth-rate does not mean a difference between a small privileged section of the rich and an undistinguished proletariat. It means a scale of fertility extending throughout the social scale. Bricklayers' labourers now contribute more to the next generation than do bricklayers; agricultural labourers more than agricultural foremen; evidence can be cited to show that in the poorest classes of industrial towns wherever inquiry is made, the most capable are found to have the fewest children.

From another aspect, the proposal for children's allowances is essentially democratic. Only by removing the premium on infertility, that is to say, the advantage of belonging to a small rather than a large family, can genuine equality of opportunity and a fair chance for ability, wherever it is found, be given. The importance of giving this equality of opportunity as between large and small families is enhanced by every development of social and educational measures designed to give greater equality of opportunity between the richer and the poorer classes. So long as the premium on infertility remains, every able boy who, by scholarships or otherwise, is given the opportunity of more important and better paid work than was performed by his father, rises into a class where he has less chance of leaving any sons behind him. The educational ladder leads today to infertility.

As there is nothing undemocratic, so there is nothing totalitarian in the proposals made here, no interference with personal liberty. A civilized community should be concerned with its own breed, as it is concerned with the breed of animals, but it should not and need not interfere with the freedom of individual citizens in the choosing of mates or the rearing of children. All that is essential is that the economic system shall no longer be such as to favour breeding from those who are less successful than from those who are more successful in rendering services to the community. Social institutions should be designed to work with nature rather than against her.

Finally, there is nothing idly visionary or remote from realities in what is suggested here. Pride of race is a reality for the British as for other peoples. Any measures taken now, by allowances for children, to stop the promotion of the infertile as well as of the able can have no immediate effect on the quality of the breed in this generation and little in the next generation. But as in Britain today we look back with pride and gratitude to our ancestors, look back as a nation or as individuals two hundred years and more to the generations illumined by Marlborough, or Cromwell, or Drake, are we not bound also to look forward, to plan society now, so that there may be no lack of men and women of the quality of those earlier days, of the best of our breed, two hundred and three hundred years hence? In the past, many a great individual has sought to perpetuate himself in a noble family. The great free people of Britain should now make sure that they will maintain their breed at its best, will have a posterity worthy of their past.

L

15

THE MASSACRE OF THE JEWS*

IN February of last year Hitler announced that "the Jews will be exterminated." Only within the past few months has it come to be generally realized outside Germany that this was no mere figure of speech, that wholesale destruction of human beings for no reason other than that they were of Jewish race had long been proceeding in some of the lands under Hitler's rule, and that in the latter part of last year the process of extermination was being organized with German thoroughness.

The House of Commons, receiving on December 17th, 1942, from the Foreign Secretary the first full and responsible statement of the facts and the declaration of protest on behalf of the United Nations, stood in silence to signalize in a way seldom, if ever, precedented, their recognition of horrors hitherto beyond belief. Mr. Eden's announcement, in declaring the condemnation by the United Nations of the bestial policy which they placed on record, proclaimed also their determination to bring retribution upon all those responsible for these crimes and to press on with the necessary practical measures to this end.

Promise of retribution was necessary and inevitable. But retribution must wait on victory, and the threat of retribution will not of itself save any lives or any pain in Germany or in lands now under German rule. No one can be content, no one is content, with threatening retribution. Since the facts were formally acknowledged in December, 1942, since they must have been known to those in authority before then, the question has become daily more insistent in the minds of all feeling men in Britain and elsewhere; what can be done to save from

* *Observer*, 7th February, 1943. *Daily Herald*, 8th February, 1943.

death and torture as many as possible of those condemned to it by the Nazi mania?

This, of course, includes persecuted people of all kinds, whatever their race. The Jews are receiving special cruelties, but do not ask for special treatment. The political martyr has as much claim on our merciful protection as the racial one. But the Jews are the largest single body of victims. What can be done to help them?

The answer to that question is not simple or very cheerful. Each of the nations that has joined in the declaration of protest at German action can, and should, revise its existing regulations for entry of refugees, so as to ensure that these cannot throw back into German hands any Jew who is able to make his escape. Knowledge that the door to safety, if it could be reached, would be found open and not barred from the other side, would no doubt encourage efforts to escape and thus increase the number of escapes. But, however much increased by this hope, the number that can make their way without special aid to any of the countries at war with Germany is trifling. The announcement made at the beginning of February 1943 by the Secretary of State for the Colonies of hastened admission to Palestine affects in the first instance refugees not from Germany itself, but from Bulgaria.

The doors of escape for most refugees lead first to some neutral country—Spain or Switzerland or Turkey. To keep those doors open as wide as possible, more positive action is required of the United Nations than a revision of their own regulations. Immediate help may be needed in feeding and transport. More important than that is a binding declaration of future policy. The thing most urgently needed to save the lives of Jews today is an announcement on behalf of the United Nations that they accept as part of their joint responsibility after victory the making of a permanent and adequate settlement of the future of Jewry in Europe and the world.

The making of such a declaration would be just. In one sense the whole war is a war about the Jewish problem. Hitler describes the war as started by Jewry to overcome the Aryan peoples. Hitler's treatment of this particular people is only the extreme case of that disregard of all human rights outside Germany which makes the Nazi creed. To destroy that creed, to re-establish the right of all human beings of all races to live unmolested while they live peaceably, is the object for which the United Nations fight. To win the war and leave the problem of Jewry unsettled for the future would be to fail in one of the objects of victory.

Threats of retribution on Germany can have little effect. The saving of lives now threatened depends upon influencing other minds than those of the Nazi leaders. First, there are Jews in peril, not only in lands directly controlled by the Nazis, but in satellite countries like Hungary and Rumania and Vichy France. To all these countries the threat of retribution, if they follow the German example, should be extended. Second, the only nations which can give first aid to any substantial numbers of Jews now threatened with destruction are the neutral nations—Spain and Switzerland and Turkey—to whose borders Jews in small numbers are escaping, to which, if the suggestion considered below for direct approach to the German rulers proved feasible, much larger numbers might come. But these neutrals cannot be expected to shoulder the whole burden of humanity. They need, first, help in feeding those who may escape; second, a firm undertaking on behalf of the United Nations that the help they give is first aid only, that the United Nations will find a permanent home elsewhere for these temporary sojourners.

When all this has been done, those who have any chance of escape while Germany pursues a policy of extermination are but a tiny fraction of all those now under threat of destruction. With a view to saving lives, not by the hundred, but by the hundred thousand, the suggestion has been made that the United Nations through the Protecting Powers should ask Germany, in place of exterminating the Jews, to set them free to leave Germany and lands under German control. This request might be refused. In that case, it is argued, no harm has been done, and, at least, every effort will have been made; the conscience of those who make the request will be clear, and the record of Germany will be blacker still. The request might receive a favourable reply; Hitler might think he saw an advantage in throwing a large mass of people upon the resources of the Allies to use their food and transport. in place of sending the inhabitants of the ghettoes to slaughter-houses in Poland and Germany, he might send them in train-loads to the borders of neutral countries and leave them there to the responsibility of the United Nations; he might use the Jews in this stage of the war as his armies used the civilian refugees of invaded countries to impede their opponents, as a weapon to stave off defeat.

Is that a reason for not making the request? That is a question which can be answered, with a full sense of responsibility, only by those who are in a position to survey the whole field of war and all its problems of feeding, transport and supply. Only by making such a request can the United Nations hope to save any large numbers of those otherwise doomed. But to make such a request and, if it met with a positive response, to fail then in rescue would have added to the present horrors the new agony of hopes raised and dashed again. All that can be said is that the possibility of making such a request must be explored fully and rejected only for conclusive reasons.

Whatever the numbers that can be saved from German fury, whether trifling as now or swollen by more vigorous efforts to escape or made a flood because Hitler's desire to embarrass his enemy outruns his hate of Jews, first-aid

to the threatened men, women, and children, depends
mainly on neutral countries. But the power and the readi-
ness of neutrals to give that aid depends on the United
Nations, for they will control the world after the war. They
alone can give a guarantee that first-aid need only be temporary and that for all those rescued today a permanent
home will be found elsewhere.

Where can this home be? What should be the ultimate
settlement of the problem of Jewry? The problem itself
is not a great one. Outside Russia there are not likely to
be in Europe after the war more than three or four
million Jews. It may be assumed that, with Hitlerism
exorcized finally from Europe, most of these could be left
or resettled as citizens of the countries to which hitherto
they have belonged. But if for their future happiness and
the peace of the world it appeared better that most Jews
should be gathered together into one community, the
finding of space for a community of this size, whether in
Europe, Asia or Africa, could not be regarded as one of
the major problems of the peace. There are many other
and more difficult problems.

But none of these things can be done by one only of
the United Nations. The refugee problem is a test both of
the humanity of all the United Nations and of their capacity
as a Grand Alliance to make up their minds upon the
problems for whose solution the Alliance exists, and in
hopes of whose solution it fights.

16

FOUR STONES FOR GOLIATH SQUALOR*

In the Report on Social Insurance and Allied Services of which, I am afraid, some of you may have heard, I urged that organization of social insurance should be treated as one part only of a comprehensive policy of social progress. Social insurance is, or should be, an attack on Want. But Want is one only of five giant evils which have to be attacked and, so far as possible, destroyed in the making of New Britain after the war. The other giant evils are Disease, Ignorance, Squalor and Idleness.

I am delighted, as well as honoured, at having been asked to open this Exhibition today because it gives me the chance of saying a few words about one of those other giants—the giant Squalor. They won't be quite so many words as the 160,000 words which I wrote recently about Want. By Squalor I mean the conditions under which so many of our people are forced to live—in houses too small and inconvenient and ill-equipped, impossible to keep clean by any reasonable amount of labour, too thick upon the ground, too far from work or country air. This Exhibition is really a declaration of war on Squalor; it points to the things which have to be done in planning town and country, and in building more and better houses, so as to make it possible for all citizens to live in an environment that is healthy, clean and pleasing to all the senses, clear of offence to sight, hearing and smell, giving easy access to work and to recreation alike. That giant Squalor is a formidable giant—far harder to attack than Want—a true Goliath. We shall not bring Goliath to

* Address on opening a "Rebuilding Britain" Exhibition at the National Gallery, 25th February, 1943.

the ground unless we carry all the necessary stones in our sling. What stones must we have?

The first stone is the planned use of land. We must be in a position to ensure that the use of all land in the country is determined according to a national plan, and not just by individual bargaining between two citizens, one owning and one meaning to use a particular piece of land. The use to which any one piece of land is put affects all the neighbours and may affect the lives of citizens over a large stretch of country. Most important of all is the use of land for the setting up of places of paid employment, whether factories or offices: population will go—must go —where employment calls it. Allowing factories and offices to be located without consideration of where the workers employed in them are to sleep or eat or shop, of where they can be entertained or educated, or of how they are to get to and from their work, has led to the disastrous, interminable growth of great cities and, in more than one case, has gone far to destroy unique historical beauty. "Planned use of land": that is a short way of putting a tremendous problem. It is easy to say, but far from easy to secure. It involves all those difficult questions as to compensation and finance which are dealt with in the Uthwatt Report and some still more difficult questions for which no solution is proposed even in that Report. Let us have no illusions about the difficulty of dealing with this issue of the use of land. But don't let us run away from the difficulty either—because without planned use of land we can't make a New Britain free from Squalor.

The second stone in our sling must be the sane use of transport. By that I mean using wisely our immense and growing means of transportation of all kinds for men and goods, our roads and railways and aircraft, using these means to spread industry and population healthily, instead of using them to jam more and more people into the great cities and their suburbs. With the sane use of transport goes also the use of power and its distribution; that, more than anything else, makes it possible to keep land to its best use—to find sites for factories, shops and houses without sacrificing farms and agriculture, without crowding all our industry around our coal-fields.

When I told a school-girl friend of mine that I was coming to open an Exhibition she said: "I hope it has a Chamber of Horrors." Well, it has. You will see many beautiful things as you go round this Exhibition and you will see some horrors also. I will mention one of these horrors only. You will see it pictured on page 38 of the book of the Exhibition, showing the plans of London drawn to the same scale at four dates, including 1914 and 1939. Please look at those plans and think what they mean. When I came first to London from Oxford to work, I went to live at Toynbee Hall in Whitechapel, and I remember that as I walked about the East End streets I used to try to imagine how many miles I and the people around me were from any pleasant country sight or sound—from real country, not a smoke-smutched open space. I remember saying to myself that if I were a super-millionaire, I'd buy up all the unbuilt land for five miles around London and stop all further building in that belt. If London wanted to go on growing, it would have to start again on the other side of the belt. That was in 1904, ten years before the map of 1914. Look at that map and at the map of 1939. How many dismal miles have been added in every direction to the distances from Whitechapel to the green! How much richer a millionaire I'd have to be to do today what I imagined nearly forty years ago!

There was a time shortly before this war when Mr. Herbert Morrison as a leading member of the London County Council was running a campaign for a green belt round London. At the same time the London Passenger Transport Board was helping to destroy green spaces round London ten times as fast as anyone could preserve

LONDON IN 1784, 1862, 1914 and 1939

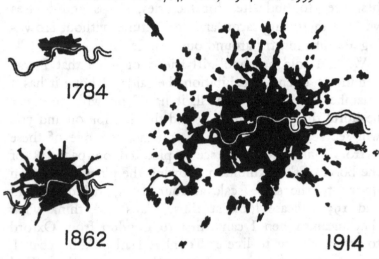

Reproduced by permission of Messrs. Lund Humphries & Co.

them; every time it opened a new station, a new green space was doomed. That is not a sane use of transport. It is not a sane use of transport to make human beings travel for two or three hours every day between their work and their dormitory suburbs rather than spread out the factories and offices and make goods or letters travel instead. It is not a sane use of transport to fix your freights so that there is an advantage in crowding together—rather than spreading out—your towns. Our second stone must be the sane use of transport and of power.

I come to the third stone: the right use of the right architects. Some of you may have been wondering why I have not mentioned architects before in opening this exhibition which they have organized. This is not because I think that what architects can do is any less important than what I've named already. It is because their job comes after those jobs in time—it comes after other people, by economic and administrative measures for the planned use of land and the sane use of transport, have brought about a reasonable distribution of industry and population. That alone provides the essential conditions within which architects as architects can work, with satisfaction to themselves and advantage to the community. Dealing with the giant Squalor is not a job for architects only or even mainly. But they have an essential part in the campaign. They must be rightly used and, as I have suggested, must be the right architects. That means that they must be architects even more concerned with the insides than with the outsides of what they design. I say that not through any under-estimate of the importance of the outside, particularly of great public buildings. One of the things of which I am most proud is that I was associated with the securing of the services of Mr. Charles Holden to design the University of London building on the site presented by the Rockefeller Foundation. The outside of that makes it one of the great buildings of the world. But there is only one University of London and there are millions of dwelling-houses and hundreds of thousands of places of paid employment, and in all these the inside is more important than the outside. It is on the ingenuity of architects that we shall depend for designing homes in which the persons who work there—that is to say, the housewives—shall have no needless toil, can have their hours of labour shortened and their health preserved. The name of Lord Shaftesbury is associated with our early Factory Laws, with measures for shortening hours and improving health in factories. Architects should set out to be the Lord Shaftesburys of the home. That means thinking not only of the walls or roof or the shape and size of the rooms, but of every detail of equipment and its placing. That means thinking of how to make homes not only well but quickly and cheaply. It is important also that those who design homes today should realize that they must be birthplaces of the Britons of the future—of more Britons than are being born today. If the British race is to continue there must be many families of four or five children. We must design houses not for the one or two child family, but houses in which large families can be expected to come into existence. The houses that we design and build today are the shell in which the British race must live, will be living for perhaps forty or fifty years. We do not want a shell so narrow or uncomfortable for numbers that it kills us. The Victorian era of nurseries without baths and garages, gave way to an era of garages and baths without nurseries. For to-morrow we can aim at all three for all—nurseries, baths and garages.

My fourth stone is the maximum efficiency of the building industry. The building industry—both managers and men—should think of themselves as about the most important industry in the country, because on how they do their work depend the lives and the happiness of citizens for many years. Houses, even the worst-built, are lasting. We cannot change them tomorrow if we do not like what we have built today, and we cannot get the houses we want without an excessive use of labour in building them unless we have also the maximum of efficiency in building to keep down its costs. A low price for a product doesn't mean low wages for the producers—as is shown by the American automobile industry; it is all a question of efficiency. A low price for a product doesn't mean that it must be ugly; machine-made simple things can be beautiful if they are made to a good design. What a low price for the product means is that every one can have more of it; cheap plenty of house-room is more important to the race than cheap motor-cars or radio. And that can come by efficiency of design and execution, by good pay to the producers for high production. I am glad that the holding of this Exhibition has been made possible by the building industry itself, which has met all the expenses involved. That is a most encouraging sign of their desire to serve the public.

These, then, are the four stones which we must put in our sling before we set out to fight the giant Squalor: planned use of land, sane use of transport, right use of the right architects and the maximum of efficiency in the building industry. But it is no use having slings or stones unless you are determined to use them: it is no use declaring war and setting out to fight unless you mean to win, unless you want passionately the things you are fighting for. The drive for dealing with the giant Squalor must come from the people of this country. What they really demand, they will get because they themselves will provide it, but they must demand it. I believe that the people of Britain desire social and economic security—freedom from Want and Idleness—so strongly that they'll be ready to pay all the price of hard work and thought involved in getting them. I hope that they are going to demand as strongly freedom from Squalor also; that they'll come to feel that the con-

ditions of crowding, discomfort, dirt, danger to health
and daily exhaustion of travelling to and from work, in
which we have been content hitherto to let so many of our
people live are not worthy of Britain or the British. If,
as a people, we come to feel that strongly enough we can
change those conditions. Now is the opportunity for
making the New Britain that we all desire.

Of course, by saying that now is the opportunity I don't
mean that now is the time to forget about the war and talk
and think chiefly about the peace. The war is not finished
yet—far from it; the winning of the war must come first
in all our thoughts and labours. Nor do I mean just the
opportunity for physical rebuilding that has been given by
the destruction of parts of some of our towns through
enemy action. Many people are talking of that, but that
opportunity is too small and uneven. The real opportunity
of the war is different and greater. The real opportunity
lies in our quickened sense of national unity, and of the
joys of fellowship and service; in having had to face so
many difficulties that seemed overwhelming and having
learned that by courage, imagination and hard work we
could overcome them. Don't let us forget those lessons.
In rebuilding Britain physically as in rebuilding it economically, socially, spiritually, let us try to carry on into the
peace the heroic mood of war.

I have pleasure in declaring this Exhibition of Rebuilding Britain open. I invite all of you who hear me, not forgetting, not letting up for a moment on the war which
we have already against that tottering ogre Hitler, to join
in declaring war upon the giant Squalor.

17

ON GOING TO AMERICA*

ONE of the pleasing points about our common language
—pleasing to ourselves though perplexing to others—is
that from the way a word is pronounced it is often impossible to tell how it should be spelt. A distinguished
Professor of Biology once started a lecture by declaring
with some pomposity that "The whole science of Biology
begins with a single cell." Whereupon a listener asked:
"Say, Mister, do you spell that last word with a 'c'
or an 's'?"

I feel that in my case also there is doubt as to spelling.
I don't mean by that the difficulty that some people have
in spelling my name or the widespread disappointment
that has resulted from the discovery that the Beveridge
of which there's so much talk is not refreshing. I mean
that I come from Oxford, and Oxford Colleges are famous
for their port. So, when your President today says that
I'm associated with one of the best sellers† in the world—
"Say, Professor Goodhart, do you spell seller with an 's'
or with a 'c'?"

The occasion of my wife and myself being here is, as
you know, that we are going to your country: at least,
we are going to your country as soon as we have been
assured of ever coming back. It doesn't seem easy to get
that assurance. Some of your Government authorities
remind me very pleasantly of the booking clerk in Los
Angeles from whom I once tried to buy a railroad ticket
East. He just wouldn't believe that I wanted a single ticket.
"No one," he said, "once he's in California takes a single
ticket away from it; they all book round trips or returns
because no one in his senses ever wants to leave for good."

* Address to American Outpost, 10th March, 1943.   † See Note 13.

So some of your authorities seem to think that no one ought to want to leave America once he's there. There's a lot to be said for that view. But, strangely enough, in leaving this country, even for yours, my wife and I want to return some time.

Why are we going to your country? Let me say at once, we're going as private citizens at the invitation of the Rockefeller Foundation, and not on behalf of the British Government. And we are not going in order to advise your President, either at his invitation or our own, as to how your country should deal with social security. He has plenty of advisers already, and very good ones. Still less am I going to urge that, if your country develops its schemes of social security, they should be based upon the scheme that I have proposed for this country. I am really not much concerned with putting over the Beveridge Report either in this country or in yours.

I'm not concerned to put over the Beveridge Report in this country because there's no need. The people of this country are going to see to that for themselves. I think they have their teeth pretty well into Freedom from Want, and when people of my country or of your country get their teeth into anything they do not loose their hold.

I'm not concerned to put over the Beveridge Report in your country, because, though I believe that the proposals of that Report suit this country, they may be wholly unsuitable for you. Though you have many of the same problems of social insecurity, it does not follow in the least that you ought to deal with them by the same methods as we adopt here. Social insurance, above all, should be national. What another country does may be very interesting to other countries, may be worth knowing about, but is certainly not a thing to copy slavishly. The social security plans of each people are part of its national culture, and should be adapted to its national tastes, like its houses, or its education, or the shapes of its women's hats, or the meaning which it attaches to the word "cracker." It's important nowadays to emphasize how much of government can and should remain purely national, in spite of the inevitable growth, as a result of this war, of international and supernational machinery. Social security in the sense in which I've used it in my Report, as income security through insurance, is of this character. It is a matter in which each nation can take its own line without ceasing to be a good neighbour to other nations.

Of course, if anyone on your side should want to know anything about the Beveridge Report, I am prepared to tell them what I know. I've a considerable pull over most people who talk about the Report. I've read it. And I do want the chance of discussing social security with those who are working at it on your side, and comparing your methods and ours. So when the Rockefeller Foundation asked my wife and myself to visit America for this purpose, she decided at once that we should go.

But it is not only social security in the narrow sense that I want to discuss in your country. Personally, I am getting rather uninterested in the Beveridge Report. My main interest now is not in social insurance or anything in the Report, but in what I have described as Assumption C of my Report, namely the assumption that by taking the requisite measures it will be possible to maintain employment in this country and avoid mass unemployment. That, next to peace itself, is the post-war problem in which the people here—and I suspect in your country, too—are more deeply interested than in anything else.

It would not have been appropriate for me in my Report to deal with this question. As I have explained elsewhere, I regard social insurance and maintenance of employment as two parts of a two-piece suit—the coat and the trousers—without both of which no man is satisfactorily dressed. But I was not asked by the Government

to design more than the trousers—that is social insurance.
Now, like a great many others in this country, I am getting
interested in the coat—that is maintenance of employment
—and as I have nothing else on hand for the Government
and as my post at Oxford gives, and is meant to give,
me time for research, I am proposing to use my time as
a private citizen to study the problem of how to maintain
employment and avoid mass unemployment in Britain
after the war.

As the first step in that study I am going to the United
States and Canada. Social insurance is a thing that each
country can do for itself. It is merely a way of re-distribu-
ting whatever wealth we have: first things first: bread for
everyone before cake for anybody. But maintenance of
employment is not a thing which any one country can
plan for itself without reference to what other countries
are likely to do. It depends on international as well as on
domestic trade; international trade in turn may be affected
by the way in which industry is organized, financed and
directed within each country. Avoidance of mass unemployment is an international problem, as clearly as
social insurance is a national one.

War and peace are indivisible. The winning of the war
must come first in all our thoughts and labours, but those
who say that the best way of winning the war is not to
think about the peace are wrong. The democracy of my
country—and, I think, of yours—have a sounder instinct.
The democracy of my country insist on being interested in
reconstruction problems and on thinking about them now.
That is partly because they realize that one fights better
if, in Cromwell's phrase, one knows what one fights for
and loves what one knows. It is partly because they have
learned by the bitter experience of the last peace that
winning a war, in the sense of reducing one's enemies to
surrender is only the first part of the job. If we don't go
on to the second part of the job—of making peace en-

during and of reconstructing prosperity for all nations—we may once again lose all the fruits of victory. We shan't do that second part of the job well unless we have thought about it beforehand. And we shan't be able to do it at all unless we go on to do it together.

Of course our continuing collaboration must extend to the political and military spheres as well as to the economic sphere. After victory itself, making peace assured and barring the way to fresh wars is our first need. Of course, also, continuing collaboration mustn't be confined to our two peoples. The contribution of all other partners of our Grand Alliance—particularly the Soviet Union and China but not forgetting the smaller nations also—will be as essential to success in peace as to success in war. What your people and mine can do to understand one another thoroughly is only a beginning, not exclusive in any way of mutual understanding between all the United Nations.

If, after the war, we are not to throw away a large part of what all of us have fought for, and for whose sake young men of all our nations have died, we must not stop collaboration too soon. We must not become dis-united nations the moment that the fighting ends. But remaining united in political and economic collaboration, till certain peace and prosperity return to the world, depends not simply or mainly on formal agreements between Governments. That is particularly true of your people and ours. You, like ourselves, are a democracy, which means that your Government, like ours, is liable to change. Continuing collaboration between countries like yours and mine cannot be secured by Atlantic Charters, signed by the Governments of today, however desirable in themselves: it must rest upon mutual understanding of one another, by the two peoples as peoples.

That is why it seems to me important that as many people as possible in this country, including myself, should understand how the main economic problems are looked at by people in your country, what views you have as to how international trade and finance should be organized, as to how much of private enterprise and how much of State control and State assistance respectively are needed, of what should be the relations between management, labour and consumers.

That's why my wife and I are going to the United States, and of course, to Canada as well, because we shouldn't want to cross the Atlantic now without visiting that part of the British Commonwealth. We want, after talking to as many people as possible on your side of the water, to be able to tell our people on this side about your attitude to post-war problems. In that way we may do something to help towards the common understanding on which alone common action can be based, and through which alone the waste and horror of war can be made into the fruitful soil of happy opportunity for all mankind hereafter. That is our hope and the reason for our journey.

18

THE PACE OF GOVERNMENT*

WITHIN three months of the presentation of my Report on Social Insurance and the Allied Services, the Government has accepted provisionally a large number of important proposals contained in it, including the introduction of children's . allowances, the establishment of a comprehensive medical service, abolition of the Approved Society system, introduction of funeral benefit, and the making of insurance comprehensive. There can be few parallels for such speed of action in peace-time, and the Government may well feel, and some of its members, no doubt, do feel, that the critics who express dissatisfaction with this achievement are unreasonable. The explanation of the dissatisfaction is that these are days not of peace but of war. The pace of government that suits peace does not suit war.

The present Prime Minister, in one of the many brilliant passages which he has added to English literature and to understanding of public affairs, has called attention to this difference, has emphasized the advantage in peace of proceeding slowly but surely by conciliation and compromise and the danger of such procedure in war. One may act too quickly in peace; to bring about reforms, however desirable in themselves, before the need for them has been accepted by public opinion generally, may lead to a revulsion, to throwing away the good that might have been gained by judicious delay. One can hardly act too quickly in the conduct of war-like operations or in the development of armed force for such operations. Here speed may more than take the place of strength. "In war," as I have written elsewhere, "the pace is set by the enemy,

* *Observer*, 21st March, 1943. *Daily Herald*, 22nd March, 1943.

not by the conversion-time of whatever may be the slowest minds in Britain."*

The importance of speed is recognized for the military side of war. It is less generally understood but equally true that war calls for a quickening and strengthening of the processes of government not for war alone, but also in preparing for its aftermath. It does so for two reasons. In the first place, tendencies to change which were in existence prior to the war may continue throughout the war, but have their practical effects suspended by the abnormal conditions of war. This can be illustrated in the history of the first war and its aftermath, by two tendencies both affecting one of our major industries : the development in other countries of sources of power alternative to coal, and the development in Britain itself of new coal-fields which could be worked more economically than the old ones. During the war any effect of these tendencies was masked; it showed itself with devastating effect on the mining industry in the aftermath. Changes of economic structure are destructive in proportion to their speed. There are some changes which happening normally would do no harm; war holds them up, like water behind a dam, to be released at its end in a destroying flood.

In the second place, there are some changes which war initiates or quickens. The first world war, compelling countries to be self-sufficient, gave an unparalleled stimulus to economic nationalism. At its end British industry and trade, trying to return to their old channels, found that the economic structure of the world had changed. Failure of the British economy under *laissez-faire* to readjust itself or to realize sufficiently the need for readjustment to changed surroundings led to mass unemployment.

War initiates or stimulates change not only in economic conditions but in public opinion. Recognition of the full

* See Paper 2 in this volume, giving the reference also to the passage mentioned from Mr. Winston Churchill's history of *The World Crisis*.

citizenship of women was a striking instance in the last war. In this war recognition of the importance of the common man, or, as it is better put, recognition of community of all classes in Britain, has been stimulated by the extremity of the general danger through which we all have passed, by the sharing of particular dangers under air attack, by the mixing of people who were formerly apart in town and country. This tendency, rightly handled, leads to national unity, not to class war. It can lead to class war and class bitterness only if it is mishandled, only if sectional interests are allowed to appear still powerful against common aims.

The end of fighting will release a double flood of change in economic conditions and popular sentiment upon this country. There will be the changes in progress before the war and held up during it. There will be changes caused or stimulated by the war itself. Plans to handle the situation positively must be ready: they cannot be ready if they are not made now.

Varying the metaphor, the need for preparedness can be put in another way. Economic and social conditions in the moment of change from war to peace will be fluid as never before or after. The ways of life of the community molten together in the crucible of war will then be released, and will begin at once to cool and harden. Will they flow into a pattern or into a shapeless mass? That depends on the mould that has been prepared beforehand for that critical moment.

The Government of today must prepare to take positive action in the immediate aftermath of war on all the main problems that will then arise—political and economic, international and domestic. This needs more strength, more courage, more imagination than in normal times. The physical courage which war calls for and produces in the people generally calls for its counterpart in moral courage on the part of the leaders, and the leaders must be ready to be leaders for peace as much as for war. It is not enough for those now in charge of our affairs to concern themselves only with the war.

To say this is not to suggest that the Government Departments are concerning themselves only with war. An immense amount of preparatory work for peace is being done. It is no doubt true, as was claimed recently by one of the Government spokesmen, that far more has been done in this war than in the last to prepare for peace. But to do no more would be a very modest ambition, after the experience of the last peace. And departmental preparation is different from Government decision. It is disturbing that on questions like physical planning of town and country, which are inter-departmental, there is so little sign of making policy—the function of the Cabinet and Parliament, not of Departments.

The strain on the Government machine at the very top is much greater in war than in peace. During the first World War this led to a fundamental change in character of the machinery at the top—to the institution of a War Cabinet of Ministers without departmental duties, to the putting of the office of Prime Minister in effect in commission. I am one of those who believe that that method was superior to anything that we have had in war government in this war and that with its adoption this time we should have reached earlier the great pitch of power and striking strength which is ours today.

To recriminate about the past is idle. But looking forward, it remains clear that the tasks of the Government in the immediate aftermath of war are overwhelming and that, if our central machinery is not strong enough to deal with those problems, we may once again lose that for which we have fought. We cannot afford the pace of peace-time, either in conducting war or in planning the next peace.

If this were peace, or if perfected social insurance were all that will be needed in the aftermath of war, most men might be more than content with what the Government

has done already on my Report, though not on othe-
Reports. But this is war, and the perfection of social inr
surance is the least and easiest of the tasks of reconstruction. To make heavy weather of plans to abolish
physical want is not encouraging of hopes of successful

WHAT, AGAIN ?

Reproduced by permission of the Proprietors of the " Evening Standard "

attack on idleness, squalor, or ignorance, to say nothing
of political and military security.

If to be strong, swift, intelligent, and decisive in planning the new world after war made it necessary to be slow
or half-hearted in the conduct of war, all men would sacrifice the lesser to the greater good, plans for peace to the
conditions of survival in war. But there is no such
necessity.

The people of Britain, fighting in the Forces, working

in fields and factories, or keeping homes and schools going, will be yet more whole of heart and mind in the struggle if they feel that, at its end, they will find something better than the chaos and frustration of the last peace. The central Government of Britain needs the same qualities for its two tasks. Strength, speed, intelligence, decision in the machine of Government are general qualities, which can be applied to problems of war and problems of its aftermath alike, if the machine is devised to develop them and to give them scope.

19

"BACK TO OUR JOB"*

THE Prime Minister's broadcast speech on the problems of peace and reconstruction was one of the major events in the war. Remarkable as it would have been at any time for its sustained vigour, scope, and eloquence, miraculous as it was from one who had so lately emerged from dangerous illness, it will owe its historic importance to things outside itself—to its setting in the course of the war, to the illustration that it affords of the working of democratic institutions.

Taken with all its warnings, that victory is not won, cannot be easy and may not be soon, the speech gives nevertheless the first vision—a break of clear seeing through driving mist and storm—of a world beyond the war. Taken with all its cautions and refusal of easy promises, and all its emphasis on keeping to our immediate tasks, it shows recognition by a great leader of democracy that democracies will have their way, in thinking even during war of peace, of planning during war for a peace that can mean a better life for all. "The people have been rendered conscious that they are coming into their inheritance."

There are particular points, of course, which one or another of those who read the speech will question or criticize. One such point is the opening warning to beware of attempts to over-persuade the Government to bind themselves or their unknown successors to great new expenditures by the State or to pledge themselves to particular schemes without relation to other schemes. This warning, if unduly regarded, might lead to a paralysis of planning.

* *Observer*, March 28, 1943. *Daily Herald*, March 29, 1943. See Note 14.

All legislation, notably any provision for pensions as of right in any form, commits the State to expenditure in the future; all borrowing by the State makes a similar commitment. And while it is true and salutary that the putting of proposals for expenditure in Parliament rests with the responsible Government of the day, it rests no less certainly with the democracy of Britain to place its needs in order of importance. If that is so, it is the right of any private citizen to endeavour to persuade the democracy to adopt that order of priority which he himself may favour and to persuade the Government to accept those priorities which he believes to accord with the wishes of the people. This right is not confined to the Chancellor of the Exchequer. In more general terms it can be urged that the Government of the day, by any of its actions or inactions, may affect the fortunes of future generations. It may affect their fortunes more harmfully by refraining from expenditure than by undertaking it.

In a very different field, doubt may be raised by the suggestion that when Hitlerism has been beaten into death, dust, and ashes, but apparently not before, the victorious Powers should "immediately begin to confer upon the future world organization." Clearly, they should have thought and, if possible, have conferred upon such matters before then. On this point, no doubt, the good answer may be given that the war today bears different aspects of urgency for different members of the United Nations, that they may not all at this moment be equally ready to confer about the future. It takes more than Britain to make a conference.

Yet another question may be asked as to the Prime Minister's suggested grouping of small nations, with its military illustration of the small nations as battalions and brigades, which are to be formed into army corps to balance other army corps. May that not merely prepare larger wars by these larger formations? Whatever be said for such groupings of small nations on other grounds, the hope of lasting peace does not lie in them. It depends on the willingness of the larger Powers to use the decisive force which they alone can develop, for the common good of enforcing order and justice among nations, and to refrain from using such force for purely national ends. It involves, as the Prime Minister indicated, the setting up of "a really effective League, with all the strongest forces concerned woven into its texture, with a High Court to adjust disputes, and with forces, armed forces, national or international or both, held ready to enforce those decisions."

Many questions of detail may be asked. The impact of the Prime Minister's speech does not depend upon its details. It depends upon devotion of so large a part of the whole, perhaps three-quarters, to problems of the Home Front after the war, to the making of a new and better Britain. This part, moreover, is couched not in generalities or in borrowed terms. Its phrases come with the force of ripe, personal conviction. It covers not one or two fields only but projects a campaign against all those giant evils —of Want, Disease, Ignorance, Squalor, and unemployment, from which, so far as possible, the Britain of the future should be free. In dealing with the last of these evils—unemployment—the Prime Minister uses more than once a phrase which must have made the Quintilians of individualism stare and gasp: "State enterprise."* By this phrase he recognizes that industry conducted by the State, that is to say, not subject to the test and motive of profit, may be enterprising. In his project of making "State enterprise and free enterprise both serve national interests and

---

* Cries the stall reader, bless us! what a word on
   A title page is this! . . .
   . . . . Why is it harder Sirs than Gordon
   Colkitto, or Macdonnel, or Galasp?
     Those rugged names to our like mouths grow sleek
     That would have made *Quintilian* stare and gasp.
        Milton: Sonnet on the book called *Tetrachordon*.

pull the national wagon side by side," he places on record a hope that the way to the practical end of ordered opportunity for all will be found along a middle course between conflicting ideologies.

In ending, the Prime Minister returns to his beginning. Having shown us for a moment through a break in the clouds a noble vision of a world after the war, he plunges into the storm again and bids the nation plunge with him. "Back to our job." That raises the question: What is "our job?" If the phrase had been not "Back to our job," but "Down to our job" there would have been no question. The job of Britain today is not simply to aid in beating Hitlerism to death, dust and ashes. The job of Britain and of all the United Nations is double: to ensure victory and then use it. War is indivisible from peace. The interest of the people of Britain in what should happen after the war is not the product of the last few months of greater success in war. It arises from the fact that most of the people are not, as the Prime Minister movingly said of himself, at a time of life when they have no personal ambitions and no future to provide for. Most of them—youngsters plunged into fighting fresh from school, young men and women balked of establishing homes and nurseries, older men and women whose careers are broken in their prime —have ambitions and futures and feel that those futures are uncertain.

Democracies will wage war better if either they know what kind of peace-time world is likely to follow upon war or if they feel that the peace-time world is being fashioned by men whom they trust for that as well as for the conduct of the war. In substance and in its proportions the Prime Minister's speech is a recognition of that fact. By turning away himself from his own advice to concentrate on the war, he has strengthened the war effort of Britain more than he could have done by any other kind of speech. He has called on the people with a new note in his voice, and he has put fresh spirit into millions; he can count on an overwhelming response from the British democracy. But to preserve that spirit and maintain that response is a task not of one night's speech, but of all the days and nights to follow.

To paint with whatever warnings a picture of the world to be is to raise hopes which it will be dangerous and weakening to dash. Over most of the field covered by the Prime Minister's broadcast, there is no reason for Britain to wait upon her Allies. There is nothing to stop the Government except themselves.* Nothing should be neglected that will ensure that the plans for peace are made and ready in time, which means for many of them that they are made and decided on in war. Nothing should be neglected that will give confidence that the plans for peace will be adequate and will be framed with sole regard to the common interest of all the people. To make and get decision on those plans in war and to give that confidence is, for the Government, part of their war job.

* See Note 15.

CHRONOLOGICAL AND OTHER NOTES

1. THE first cartoon refers to the Report of the Committee on Skilled Men in the Services which had been appointed on 9th June, 1941, and after an Interim Report, in September, 1941, made its definite Report on 31st October, 1941. The Committee, in addition to myself, as Chairman, consisted of Mr. George Bailey, at that time President of the Engineering Employers' Federation, Mr. J. C. Little, formerly President of the Amalgamated Engineering Union, and Mr. R. G. Simpson. The terms of reference to the Committee required it to

> "examine in consultation with the three Service Departments, the use now made in the Royal Navy, the Army and the Royal Air Force of skilled men and to advise in the light of the operational and maintenance commitments of the three Services:—
>
> (*a*) whether the skilled man-power already at the disposal of the Services is being used with due economy and effect;
>
> (*b*) whether the Service arrangements for training skilled men are such as to meet to the greatest practicable extent the Service requirements for skilled men;
>
> (*c*) whether the demands of the Services for skilled men as recruits to Service trades during the period ending 31st March, 1942, should in any respect be modified."

The Committee, from an analysis of lists of men supplied by employers and trade unions followed by visits to military establishments of all kinds and a number of personal interviews, reported that "the extent to which men of rare skill find that skill unused in the Forces remains disturbing and surprising. It is the more surprising in view of the vigorous efforts made in all three Services . . . to bring about a remustering and using of men according to their skill. These efforts have been almost continuous since the early days of war." The extent of this failure to use skill fully, both absolutely and relatively to the total numbers was markedly greater in the Army than in either of the other Services; the Committee named a number of factors making "adjustment of supply to demand and full use of skilled men harder for the Army than it is for either of the other Services or . . . for civilian industry." The Committee emphasized the character of their enquiry as an audit: "every audit shows errors which must be judged with a due sense of proportion."

The Report of the Committee was published on 18th February, 1942, with a Memorandum of reply by the War Office.

Two major changes of Army organisation recommended in the Report were:—

(a) that "men should be enlisted not into this or that corps of the Army, but into the Army as a single Service as they are taken into the Royal Navy or into the Royal Air Force and that being examined at centres common to the whole Army, they should from those centres be posted to their definite Corps only when it is clear that they fit the requirements of those Corps and that any scarce skill possessed by them will be turned fully to account," and

(b) that there should be established in the Army a Corps of Mechanical Engineers.

Both of these proposals, as stated in the Report, had been under consideration by the Army Authorities at one time or another in the past. Both have now been adopted.

General enlistment has been in force since 2nd July, 1942. All men are enlisted for the first six weeks into a "General Service Corps" and are posted to their definite Corps thereafter in the light of their suitability for the work that they will be required to do and having regard to the estimate of the numbers of men of each type of skill required by the different Corps, based on a full "job analysis" of the work to be done by each Corps. This "job analysis," an essential preliminary to the present process of sorting men, had been begun at the same time as the Committee on Skilled Men in the Services was appointed; it required ten months' work.

The other major recommendation named above has been carried into effect by the setting up of "R.E.M.E.", that is to say, the Corps of Royal Electrical and Mechanical Engineers. Many other recommendations of the Committee, affecting not only the Army but also the Royal Navy and the Royal Air Force, have also been carried into effect.

2. The Parliamentary Debate referred to at the beginning of Paper 1 took place on 27th and 29th January, 1941, and ended in a vote of confidence in the Government by 464 votes to 1 vote. The appointment of Lord Beaverbrook as Minister of War Production was announced on 4th February, 1942.

3. The changes in the Government referred to at the beginning of Paper 2 include the addition to the War Cabinet on 19th February, 1942, of Sir Stafford Cripps as Lord Privy Seal and Captain Oliver Lyttelton as Minister of State charged with the duty of "exercising general supervision over production." At the same time Lord Beaverbrook, though invited to remain a member of the Government, left it.

4. On the date of publication of Paper 2, that is 17th March, 1942, Mr. Dalton, as President of the Board of Trade, announced the decision of the Government to introduce fuel rationing and that I had been invited to report on the method of rationing, in the following terms: "Mere exhortations were not enough. The Government had decided that a comprehensive scheme of fuel rationing should be introduced as soon as possible. He had invited Sir William Beveridge to report to him on the most effective and most equitable method of restricting and rationing the consumption of fuel and power." In accordance with this invitation, I made a Report on 13th April, 1942, which, after some revision in consultation with Mr. Dalton and his officials, was presented in final form on 19th April and published on 28th April, 1942, as Cmd. 6352.

The Report contained an outline scheme of comprehensive fuel rationing on a points system with interchangeable coupons, introduced by a memorandum in which the difficulties of such rationing were pointed out. "Fuel rationing presents materially greater difficulties than food rationing. It cannot be expected to work so smoothly. While I am satisfied that the special difficulties of fuel rationing can be overcome, these difficulties must be faced before a decision to ration is undertaken. There remains the difficulty of staff—a difficulty common now to all extensions of Government activity."

In announcing the receipt of this Report on 21st April, 1942, Mr. Dalton again stated that the Government had decided to introduce fuel rationing. This announcement produced an explosion of objections in Parliament, and after the subject had been debated in the House of Commons on 7th May, 1942, fuel rationing was first postponed and then allowed to fade out by stages. On 3rd June it was announced that Major Gwilym Lloyd George had been appointed to the new office of Minister of Fuel and

Power—taking over the Ministry of Mines and those parts of the Board of Trade which had been concerned with this before. Ultimately, it was found possible to avoid fuel rationing: it seems probable that economies in the industrial use of coal, voluntary restriction by householders and the mild winter, in that order of importance, have been the main factors contributing to this result. In the course of the Parliamentary Debate on 8th May I was accused of frivolity for having made a Report on fuel rationing in a month. In a letter published in *The Times* on 14th May I tried to defend myself against this charge by pleading that this was the pace at which we learnt to work for victory in the last war.

5. "Look What's Going In," published on 24th November refers on the one hand to the announcement by Sir Stafford Cripps as Lord Privy Seal on 17th November, 1942, that my Report on Social Insurance and Allied Services was expected to be published about the end of the month, and on the other hand, to the announcement on the 23rd November that Sir Stafford Cripps had left the War Cabinet in order to take up the post of Minister of Aircraft Production.

6. *The Report on Social Insurance and Allied Services* signed by me on 20th November, 1942, was printed with extreme expedition and presented to Parliament as a Command Paper (Cmd. 6404) on 1st December, 1942, advance copies having been supplied to the Press confidentially on 27th November. The Report, with Appendices A to F, was placed on sale for 2/- with a companion volume of memoranda from Organizations (Cmd. 6405) also sold for 2/-. I gave a broadcast address in the Empire Service on the evening of 1st December and substantially repeated this on the following evening in the Home Service address which is printed here as Paper 6.

I made the Report as Chairman of an Inter-Departmental Committee appointed in June 1941 by Mr. Arthur Greenwood, as Minister without Portfolio charged with the general supervision of reconstruction plans. In January 1942 it was decided that the Report should be made and signed only by me and not by the departmental representatives. By the time that the Report was made, Mr. Arthur Greenwood had been succeeded as Minister concerned with reconstruction plans by Sir William Jowitt, holding the office of Paymaster-General. My Report was submitted accordingly to Sir William Jowitt who figures in the cartoon on page 111.

7. The title given to Paper 7 refers to the fact that two previous attempts to get the contents of the paper into circulation proved unsuccessful. It was prepared in the first instance (on 17th November, 1942) as a summary of my coming Report on Social Insurance and Allied Services with a view to its distribution to the Press, particularly overseas, to enable them to deal with the Report. I thought that a summary by myself would be most likely to ensure that the points of greatest importance received the greatest attention. The Ministry of Information decided to make their own summary. I was relieved by this, because my summary thus became available to meet requests which I had received from the Army Bureau of Current Affairs for material to be circulated for distribution in the Army. I placed my summary at the disposal of the Army Bureau of Current Affairs for this purpose and they printed it in a Bulletin with some changes approved by me and an introduction which I did not see. Later, the Bulletin was withdrawn. I print my summary here because I believe that it is still the best short account of what I intended and a useful guide to the study of the Report. It is not possible from the summary to form any judgment on the controversy aroused by the withdrawal of the Army

Bureau of Current Affairs Bulletin after it had been printed and distributed, since that differs from the summary both in certain omissions and by addition of the introduction. I do not print it as in any way a contribution to that controversy. *Suave mari magno.* I have been able to contemplate this particular controversy from the outside without having to form an opinion on its merits, though not, I imagine, without the gain which in Britain accrues naturally to any author from anything which rightly or wrongly looks like banning of any of his works. I should add that, though this is the first appearance, as a whole, of my summary of my Report, it has appeared in part as an article in the February number of *Britain Today*, published by the British Council.

8. The first of the few speeches which I made in explanation of my Report, in face of a demand for speeches from nearly every town of any size in the country, was made at a Public Interest Defence Luncheon at the Savoy Hotel on 9th December, 1942. As some of the points made in this speech do not appear so definitely elsewhere in this volume, the main points are given briefly from the notes from which I spoke.

9. Paper 11 was published just before the House of Commons debated my Report for three days on 16th–18th February, 1943, and Paper 12 in two articles shortly after. The debate took place on a Resolution moved by Mr. Arthur Greenwood, Leader of the Labour Party, in the following terms :—

> "That this House welcomes the Report of Sir William Beveridge on Social Insurance and Allied Services as a comprehensive review of the present provisions in this sphere and as a valuable aid in determining the lines on which developments and

legislation should be pursued as part of the Government's policy of post-war reconstruction."

This Resolution was seconded by a Conservative member in a speech largely devoted to traversing the arguments of the proposer of the Resolution. After the Government's attitude had been explained by Sir John Anderson on the first day of the debate, an amendment was put down by Mr. James Griffiths, Mr. Shinwell and other members of the Labour Party expressing "dissatisfaction with the now declared policy of His Majesty's Government towards the Report of Sir William Beveridge," and urging "reconsideration of that policy with a view to the early implementation of the plan." After the Government attitude had been re-stated by the Chancellor of the Exchequer (Sir Kingsley Wood) and the Home Secretary (Mr. Herbert Morrison) on the second and third days of the debate, the Amendment was defeated by 335 votes to 119 votes, by two or three votes the largest number recorded up to that time against the present Government. Immediately after the voting I happened to find myself taking part in a Trans-Atlantic discussion of Social Security in which some of my interlocutors were interested to know my reaction to the debate. I said that, if they wished to know how I would have voted on the amendment, since I was not a member of the House, I fortunately was not under obligation to vote either way.

10. Governments had no need to remain ignorant until publication of the prospective contents of Reports, either in 1909 or in 1942. As is stated in the account of the origin of unemployment insurance and Labour Exchanges which I gave in 1930, the "remarkable celerity" shown by the Government of 1909 "in acting on the recommendations of a Royal Commission had its explanation and was not the fruit simply of three months of thought."

"Six months before the Report was issued, though not in ignorance of its prospective contents, Mr. Churchill had obtained the assent of his colleagues to establishing a national system of Labour Exchanges. He had at the same time asked certain officials of the Board of Trade to devise if they could a scheme of unemployment insurance. . . .

"On 19th May, 1909, Mr. Winston Churchill, as President of the Board of Trade, announced the intention of the Government to introduce compulsory insurance against unemployment. The project seemed then and was a daring adventure. Except for one ill-judged and disastrous experiment in the Canton of St. Gall, compulsory insurance against unemployment had never been attempted in any country of the world. All voluntary schemes had been immediate failures or insignificant successes. The only working model on a large scale was afforded by trade unions, which undertook no legal liabilities, were armed with almost indefinite powers of raising levies, and consisted predominantly of the picked members of skilled trades. Germany, which had led the way in accident and sickness insurance twenty-five years before, was still hesitant as to the possibility of defining insurable unemployment and testing whether it had occurred. . . .

"The birth of compulsory unemployment insurance is a signal instance of how much the personality of a single Minister in a few critical months may change the course of social legislation. It may be cited also to illustrate the initiative of Civil Servants. The chief official concerned—Sir Hubert Llewellyn Smith, then Permanent Secretary of the Board of Trade—happened in 1910 to be President of the Economic Section of the British Association, and took the occasion in his Presidential Address to analyse the problem of unemployment insurance and, incidentally, expound the principles underlying the scheme which he with others was framing."*

This Presidential Address, printed in large part in the *Economic Journal* for December, 1910, and briefly summarized by me in the work just cited, has historical importance as a record of the hopes, anxieties and purposes with which compulsory unemployment insurance came into the world. In his radio address of 21st March, 1943, Mr. Winston Churchill justly emphasized the leading part played by Sir Hubert Llewellyn Smith.

The celerity of Government decision on the Report of the Poor Laws Commission in 1909 was even greater than is suggested in Paper 12, or in the quotation given above from my study of *Unemployment*. The Report of the Commission was signed on 4th February, 1909, and first published in the press on 18th February. The King's Speech made at the opening of Parliament on 16th February, that is before its publication, referred to this Report and stated that "a measure will be proposed for the better organisation of the labour market through a system of co-ordinated labour exchanges with which other schemes for dealing with unemployment may subsequently be associated." The first announcement that these "other schemes" would include compulsory contributory insurance against unemployment was made, not in Mr. Churchill's speech of 19th May, 1909, but three weeks before by Mr. Lloyd George as Chancellor of the Exchequer, in introducing the Budget on 29th April. The Government of 1909 had in fact decided on a policy for unemployment before the Report of the Commission was published, and even before it was signed, though with full knowledge of what it was likely to contain.

* *Unemployment: A Problem of Industry* (1909 and 1930), pp. 262–4 (Published in 1930).

Mr. Churchill left the Board of Trade to become Home Secretary in February 1910, and the actual introduction of unemployment insurance as Part II of the National Insurance Bill of 1911 was undertaken by his successor, Mr. Sydney Buxton. There was in those days no Ministry of Labour (established at the end of 1916). In explaining in May 1909 why Labour Exchanges and unemployment insurance fell to the Board of Trade, Mr. Churchill said: "The Board of Trade is concerned with the organisation of industry, so far as the Government may properly concern itself with the organisation of industry." This observation may be compared with the references to State enterprise in Mr. Churchill's broadcast of 21st March, 1943. The world has moved.

11. In Paper 12 as first published I gave the proportion of the total increase of £174 millions that resulted from increased proportion of old people and inclusion of new classes as "hardly less than half" and the proportion due to making pensions rise in scale by consequence as "only half." I reached these proportions by use of the Registrar-General's estimates of the persons of pensionable age as given in Table XI of my Report. The Government Actuary, however, has made slightly different assumptions from the Registrar-General as to the future course of mortality in old age and by consequence has allowed for a smaller total number of pensioners in 1965 than is suggested in Table XI. On the assumption made by the Government Actuary and leading to his total of £174 millions increase, the proportion of this increase due to the rising scale of pensions appears to be about three-fifths rather than half and the proportion due to increase and proportion of old people and inclusion of new classes is about two-fifths. I have used these proportions accordingly in the paper as now printed.

The figures of £325 millions as the cost of pensions on

my plan and £265 or only £60 millions less as the cost of pensions on a 30/- basis relate to the first year after the end of the transition period assumed as 1965. For two reasons the difference between the costs of the two proposals will rise somewhat after 1965: first, through increase in the total number of pensioners: second through all the new classes of pensioners becoming entitled to the full 40/- on my plan. The chance of being able to keep pensions down to 30/- or to any point substantially below unemployment and disability benefit is in practice so small as to make this comparison academic. Sir John Anderson himself spoke of the definite rate of pension preferred by the Government remaining only till Parliament decided to change it. This is a direct invitation to political auction.

12. Under a long-standing engagement I delivered the Galton Lecture to the Eugenics Society on 16th February, 1943, the afternoon of the first day of the Parliamentary Debate upon my Report. This lecture has been printed in the *Eugenics Review* from a shorthand note. Paper 14 printed here is an article not previously published, written in the course of preparing for this lecture.

13. My Report on Social Insurance and Allied Services is easily the best seller to date among British official Reports (about 250,000 of the full Report, 350,000 of the official abridgement and 42,000 of the American Edition). The previous best seller, I believe, was the Report of the Royal Commission on the Coal Industry under the Chairmanship of Viscount Samuel in 1926. This Report was placed on sale for 3d., had a sale of about 100,000 copies, and was followed by the General Strike. I was a member of the Commission—on the invitation of Mr. Winston Churchill then Chancellor of the Exchequer.

14. The Prime Minister's speech, which is the subject of Paper 19, was broadcast on Sunday, 21st March, 1943.

The principal passages in the speech (other than those quoted fully in the Paper itself) to which my comment is relevant are as follows :—

" . . . my earnest advice to you is to concentrate even more zealously upon the war effort, and if possible not to take your eye off the ball even for a moment. If tonight, contrary to that advice, I turn aside from the course of the war and deal with some post-war and domestic issues, that is only because I hope that by so doing I may simplify and mollify political divergences, and enable all our political forces to march forward to the main objective in unity and, so far as possible, in step.

.   .   .

"The business of proposing expenditure rests ulti-mately with the responsible Government of the day, and it is their duty, and their duty alone, to propose to Parliament any new charges upon the public and also to propose in the annual Budgets the means of raising the necessary funds.

.   .   .

"I personally am very keen that a scheme for the amalgamation and extension of our present incom-parable insurance system should have a leading place in our Four Years' Plan. . . . Here is a real oppor-tunity for what I once called 'bringing the magic of averages to the rescue of the millions.' Therefore, you must rank me and my colleagues as strong partisans of national compulsory insurance for all classes for all purposes from the cradle to the grave.

.   .   .

"The future of the world is to the highly educated races who alone can handle the scientific apparatus necessary for pre-eminence in peace or survival in war.

.   .   .

"It is therefore necessary to make sure that we have projects for the future employment of the people and the forward movement of our industries carefully foreseen, and, secondly, that private enterprise and State enterprise are both able to play their parts to the utmost.

.   .   .

"I end where I began. Let us get back to our job. I must warn every one who hears me of a certain—shall I say?—unseemliness and also of a danger of it appearing to the world that we here in Britain are diverting our attention to peace, which is still remote, and to the fruits of victory, which have yet to be won, while our Russian allies are fighting for dear life and dearer honour in the dire, deadly, daily struggle against all the might of the German military machine, and while our thoughts should be with our armies and with our American and French comrades now engaged in decisive battle in Tunisia."

.   .   .

15. In saying in the final paragraph of Paper 19 that "there is nothing to stop the Government except themselves" in making plans for domestic reconstruction, I am recalling an observation made by Mr. Winston Churchill in a famous speech on 17th November, 1916, when he was criticizing the Government of that day for not proceeding fast enough in making total war and controlling the lives of all citizens. "Why not do these now? . . . No one is stopping the Government except themselves."

ACKNOWLEDGMENTS

ABOUT one-third of the contents of this volume represents articles which have appeared in the weekly or daily papers named in each case. They are printed substantially in their original form, with minor trimmings to suit them for presentation in a volume. Most of the rest is now printed for the first time. The two radio addresses are printed as they were read and two of the shorter addresses (Nos. 16 and 17) which were either broadcast or prepared for broadcasting are also printed practically as they were delivered. None of the other addresses were written out before delivery; they were given from relatively brief notes. One of them—the address on "New Britain" at Oxford—was recorded as given, with a view to broadcasting, and with a little editing and clarification is printed from a typescript prepared from the recording. I am much obliged to the British Broadcasting Corporation for placing this typescript at my disposal. In one case (No. 8) I have printed no more than the notes from which I spoke. The other addresses, namely 4, 5 and 13, have been reconstructed from the short notes from which they were spoken, having been re-dictated for the purpose of printing. So far as my memory served I have reproduced faithfully what I said or meant to say.

Two of the written papers have not appeared previously. One of them (No. 7) is my own Summary of my Report on Social Insurance and Allied Services, a part of which was published as an article in *Britain Today*. The other (No. 14) is a memorandum on Children's Allowances and the Race, written in connection with the preparation of notes from which I delivered the Galton Lecture at the Eugenics Society on 16th February, 1943.

I have to acknowledge the kindness of Mr. Spencer

Summers in allowing me to re-print his half of Paper 11,
and of the editors of the various papers in which my
articles first appeared. I am grateful for the permission
accorded to me of illustrating my text by a number of
cartoons which appeared during the period of the papers
in the *Evening Standard*, in *Punch* and the *News Chronicle*,
and by a plan from the Exhibition which I opened on
"Rebuilding Britain."

My greatest debt is naturally to Mr. Low, who has
allowed me to use no less than six of his cartoons; I
count myself fortunate in thus being able to enlist his
enlivening aid. Two of Mr. Low's cartoons have to me
the special interest of recalling activities which do not
appear in my papers but are described briefly in the notes.
They relate respectively to the Committee on Skilled Men
in the Services whose preparations formed my principal
occupation from the beginning of June, 1941, to the end
of October, 1941, and to the Fuel Rationing scheme which
absorbed me even more completely from the middle of
March, 1942, to the latter part of April. These were both
interludes in the preparation of the Report on Social
Insurance and Allied Services which was spread over
seventeen months from the appointment of the Inter-
departmental Committee, announced on 10th June, 1941,
to the signature of the Report on 20th November, 1942.

In so far as I am using Crown copyright material either
in actual quotations from my Report on Social Insurance
and Allied Services or in the summary thereof I am doing
so with the permission of the Controller of H.M. Stationery
Office.

W. H. B.

LARGE OR SMALL NATION? A POSTSCRIPT*

Two recent events have called attention to the problem of the birth-rate. One is the publication at the beginning of April 1943 of the Return of the Registrar-General for England and Wales, giving statistics of births, deaths, and marriages in the year 1942. The other is the reference made to this problem by the Prime Minister in his broadcast speech of 21st March, 1943.

The Registrar-General has recorded that the number of births in England and Wales in 1942 was 655,000, nearly 68,000 more than in 1941, the highest number born in any year since 1928. Does this mean that the tendency to a dwindling birth-rate has been reversed? Does it mean, what is more important, that there are now sufficient births to prevent the threatened decline of the population of Britain? The answer to both of these questions is negative.

The Registrar-General's Return deals with marriages also. It shows that the number of marriages in 1940 was a record for all time, and the number in 1941 was also higher than in any previous year except the boom years of 1919 and 1920 after the last war. Most marriages lead to at least one birth, and therefore an increase of the marriage rate leads naturally to an increase of the birth-rate one or two years after. For reasons arising out of the last war, the number of young adult women in Britain—particucularly those born in 1920 or just before or after and now aged twenty-two or twenty-three—is exceptionally large. For reasons connected with this war they have had more than the usual opportunity for marrying, through the filling of Britain with armed forces, and through the war boom in employment. The recent increase of marriages is the result of special circumstances and cannot be maintained. It is more than enough to account for the increase of births.

* *The Observer*, 11th April, 1943.

Reversal of the existing tendency of the birth-rate and escape from the position in which the British people find themselves—that they are not replacing themselves for the future—cannot be brought about simply by an increase in marriages, unless there are more children to each marriage. The Registrar-General's Return is no evidence of such prospective increase in the average number of children to each marriage. Unless that average number can be raised, the present generation of Britons will not replace itself in the next generation and that generation will not replace itself in the generation after. The numbers of the British people will fall steadily.

Is that to be regarded as a disaster, or a good result, or as something to be accepted with indifference? Britain as a whole is already one of the most densely populated countries of the world. Ought we to regret the prospects of a diminution of numbers and to take steps to stop that diminution? Is it essential to British civilization that the British nation should continue to be a large nation?

The first stage in answering that question is to admit that the civilization of a people does not depend upon its size. In all stages of human history relatively small nations have contributed to the general civilization of the world as notably as large nations. Tiny Attica has meant more than all the hosts of Persia. To-day human life may be as full and as well worth living in a community of five millions as in a community of fifty millions—on one condition: that the small community is allowed to live in peace.

The purpose of the peace settlement of 1919 was described by one of its authors as making the world safe for democracy. Without any surrender of belief in democracy, it may be suggested that for the next peace settlement the purpose should be phrased differently: to make the world safe for small nations. That means making it a world ruled by justice among nations as well as within nations, with a sanction of force behind the justice. It

means a world in which the rights of an individual citizen
are not greater because he belongs to a large nation rather
than to a small nation. But all this in turn depends on
some nations being both large and just.

> O it is excellent
> To have a giant's strength; but it is tyrannous
> To use it like a giant.

If peace, justice and happiness are to return to mankind,
there must be some nations which have a giant's strength
but will not use it like an ogre.

To be one of those large nations, loving peace and
accepting and enforcing justice, should be Britain's role.
To fulfil that role, as the Prime Minister said, the British
people must keep up their numbers. Had the British
population between the Napoleonic Wars and the first
World War grown at the same slow rate as the French
population grew in that period, the German people in
1914 would have outnumbered the peoples of Britain and
France together, and the result of the first World War
would almost certainly have been different. Had the
British population in Victorian days, as the Prime Minister
said, not risen to the level of a Great Power "we might
have gone down the drain with many other minor States
to the disaster of the whole world. If, therefore, this
country is to keep its high place in the leadership of the
world and to survive as a Great Power that can hold its
own against external pressure, our people must be encouraged by every means to have larger families."

The British people as a people are faced to-day by need
for a great decision. Will they be a large nation or a small
nation? That is the issue. To-day the British people are
headed for the second alternative of being small: the
latest Return of the Registrar-General is no evidence at
all of any reversal of direction. If for to-morrow a different
direction—of remaining large—is desired, a change to

larger families is essential. How can that change be brought about?

It can follow only from a change of public opinion. It cannot be brought about by any system of economic rewards; people will not have children for pay. Pronouncements such as those made by the Prime Minister are the most practical contribution—an indispensable first step—to the maintenance of our numbers.

But if a change of public opinion in favour of larger families is the first step, economic and social measures designed to remove the disadvantages of such families are an indispensable practical supplement.

The most obvious and simple of these measures is provision of children's allowances—on an adequate scale and not as the Government have proposed them. People will not have children for pay. But there must be many parents with one or two children who would like more children and hesitate now for fear of damaging the prospects and opportunities of those they have already. There might be many more parents who would feel like this, if the national importance of increasing the average size of families came to be nationally recognized. Our economic system to-day involves inequalities of opportunity, not only between classes but between the children of small and the children of large families in every case. If children's allowances are to be effective in remedying this inequality, they must be adequate: they must be enough for subsistence in every case, and should be supplemented by special schemes for particular occupations.

Another set of obvious measures are those concerned with the safeguarding of maternity—by free comprehensive medical service—and with provision for its special costs. These measures also are relatively easy of accomplishment, once the need is seen.

Yet a third set of measures, as important but not so easy, are those concerned with housing. The houses that will be built in the ten or twenty years after the war are the shell in which the British people will have to live for forty or fifty years after. Who is going to design those houses and under what instructions? Are they going to be homes—in situation, size, equipment—in which the burden of bringing the next much larger generation of Britons into the world can reasonably be undertaken, in which this burden will freely be undertaken by men and by women who are free to choose?

INDEX

NATIONAL ASSISTANCE, 63.
NATIONAL MINIMUM—
in relation to health, 57, 84;
Security Plan part of, 82;
abandoned by Government, 132,
144;
priority for, 135–6, 149;
British idea, 143, 148.
NELSON'S SIGNAL, 29.
"NEW ORDER," 97.
NEW ZEALAND—
pensions precedent, 55, 69, 146;
security financed by taxation, 123.

OSBORN, FREDERICK, 157.
OXFORD COLLEGES, 175.

PARLIAMENT, BRITISH, preferable to
alternatives, 91.
PARTY, place of, 23.
PEACE, see War.
PENSIONS—
proposals in Report, 54–5, 63,
68–9, 127, 131, 146–7;
contributory, introduced by Conservatives, 77;
Government proposals criticized,
127–31, 144–6, 202–3.
PLAN FOR SOCIAL SECURITY, 53–75
(summarized 60–4);
contribution to victory, 10;
part of comprehensive programme,
10, 71, 77;
three sides, 53;
relation to Atlantic Charter, 53,
58, 71;
cost, 57, 73, 123–4, 136, 140;
re-distributes income, 60, 76, 113;
principles; 60, 127,
contributory principle, 70, 123,
146–7;
a British revolution, 71;
neither socialism nor capitalism,
77;
provisions compared with pre-war
provision, 74–5;
puts first things first, 77, 103, 148;
on British lines, 77–8;
contribution to common cause, 78;
assumptions of, 98;
abolition of want as aim, 132.
PLANNING, NATIONAL, meaning and
need for, 45–9.
POOR LAWS AND RELIEF OF DISTRESS,
Royal Commission on, 126, 201.
POPE PIUS XII, 33.
PRICE, every good thing has, 50.
PRICE MECHANISM, 45, 47.

QUINTILIANS OF INDIVIDUALISM, 189.

R.E.M.E. (CORPS OF ROYAL ELECTRI-
CAL AND MECHANICAL ENGIN-
EERS), 193–4.
RENT, problem of, 130.
ROCKEFELLER FOUNDATION, 171, 176,
177.
RUSSIA, 22, 31, 45, 88, 149; see
Soviet Union.

SAVING, Obligation of, 34, 122.
SCOTT REPORT, 86.
SECURITY, see Plan for Social Security.
SERVICE, not gain as motive, 22, 39.
SHAFTESBURY, LORD, 172.
SHINWELL, E., 199.
SHIPPING FEDERATION, 142.
SICKNESS, higher rate allowed for,
101.
SIMPSON, R. G., 192.
SKILLED MEN IN SERVICES, Committee on, 9, 78, 192–4, 208.
SMITH, SIR HUBERT LLEWELLYN,
200, 201.
SOCIAL INSURANCE—
nature of, 66;
not party question, 77, 89, 106;
easiest of reconstruction tasks, 89,
185;
can differ for different countries,
113, 176, 178;
as trousers, 139–40, 146, 177–8;
see Plan for Social Security.
SOCIAL INSURANCE AND ALLIED
SERVICES, Committee on, 42,
59, 77.
SOCIAL INSURANCE AND ALLIED
SERVICES, Report on—
preparation, 9;
signature, 10, 59;
action by Government, 126 seq.,
181;
not one-man, 141–3;
sales, 175–203;
publication, 196;
debate on, 198–9.
SOCIAL SECURITY, MINISTRY OF, 64,
70, 133–4.
SOVIET UNION, 34, 179; see Russia.
SQUALOR, 167–74;
meaning, 43, 85;
methods of dealing with national,
113–14;
drive against, must come from
people, 173.
STATE—
control of industry and incomes
urged, 22;
as general parent, 38;
use of power, 90;
enterprise, 189.

Printed in the United States
by Baker & Taylor Publisher Services

EPILOGUE

THE LOVER

LOVE NOTES FROM THE UNIVERSE

DIVINE FAMILIAR

I had a name for you once;
it seemed to fit,
when I scarcely knew you –
who you were,
what you were.
Unbeknownst to me then,
you had so many names,
you had so many faces.

Chimerical and powerful,
soft and steady, that you were;
I tried these names all so familiar,
but no human calling was complete
in summing up your everything,
with such a common sound or two,
how could that ever, ever do?
in serving to define
your Great All-Energy, and
everything you are to me –
Divine

DREAM A LITTLE DREAM

The dream was real;
my body believed it,
still humming and now
still grasping for you.

Tossed ruthlessly to Earth,
your lips torn from mine,
blood afire like turpentine-
lit and vanished in a flash,
now awake, empty and dazed
but sure I just crossed time and space
with you wrapped around me,
so tell me please -
how could this be
just a dream
just a little, little
little dream?

CONSPIRACY

Make no mistake:
the worlds have conspired
to match each circumstance
of infinite time and space
for us to be together
Now.

FACES OF YOU

Each time I see you,
you are born anew;
never the same view
to me!

Upside down,
I see you now;
looking back at me
so serene,
then giggling –
or sober and stern
from challenging concerns;
not the same face at all
today from yesterday,
and tomorrow what will play
on my eyes,
on my mind,
on my heart?

RIPPLES AND WAVES

Precious, priceless face,
finest art of all;
your voice is my music,
your presence so soothing,
calming and smoothing
the ripples of my soul.

All my worries and
indeed, my existence,
quiet and fade
as I lie ear to cage,
and hear without hearing
all worldly solutions and
secrets for peace
being spelled out in code,
in melodious mode,
by the rhythmic hammering
of your beautiful heart,
making happy new waves
today in my soul.

WE

If only I could fold up your essence,
and tuck you into a suitcase;
indeed, then I would take you
every place.

I could wheel you around,
town to town,
over land and over sea,
you'd go everywhere with me
and I would never be
I or me,
but forever us,
together –
We.

EYE SIGH

Amber amulets hung side by side
are your eyes in bright sunlight,
but in shadows bake
into molten maple syrup
in the sweet stack of your face.

Twin shots of warm cognac,
drunk from your gaze,
spread cozy heat in ardent waves
but in neither darkness nor in light,
your eyes cannot deny
their luminous reflection
of this world's perfection –
I sigh!

SUMMATION

She was everything,
She had everything,
and He was everything
to Her.

All She could ever want,
ever dream to behold,
was Hers thanks to Him –
Him who adored Her.

Him for whom
She gave everything;
He was the treasure,
He treasured everything.
She became everything
to Him.

TWIN SOULS

She was drowning and
his lips brought the first taste of air;
as she breathed in his essence,
nothing compared.
It drove her to claw
and grab for the source
of inebriating vapor
and now drink and savor
more of his feast
that fueled her awake
and alive in 5-D.

She presses, interlopes,
but their skin hateful barriers,
chaining them, barring passage.
She hums from her core,
and a vibrating energy
penetrates through his pores:
they are separate no more.
Recognition floods through,
what was thought to be two,
and decidedly melts that illusion.

WICKED MOON

Wicked moon, glowing full,
always rousing me from slumber!
Willing me to wake and write,
willing me to walk the night –
compelled to rise, and go outside,
as though I hear my Romeo
calling William's verses
from high above my window,
not below,
but I must go –
under the sky, out to greet him,
in his fullness and completeness!
A siren's call heard by my soul,
and for one moment in his glow,
I am sure of all I know
and all is all is all
is well
below.

FORMIDABLE YOU

Who can imagine the You I know?
How incredibly lovely and soft
the silky pink underside is –
the hidden belly of this,
most untouchable beast.

RIVER MEETS SEA

Life-giving water pulses ahead
where River meets Sea,
determined to reach her,
to breach her
estuary.

A trove of gems and silken silt
lay left behind each previous time;
sharp rocks and smooth sand,
the calling card of every man.

His fresh current penetrates,
purposefully moving,
mixing into her boundless depths,
convincing her that
she could be more
than ever before,
and delightfully less salty.

SHHHHHH

In the dark,
I see you better
and hear you so well
in the silence
I know you best,
right here and now –
shhhhhh

SOMETIME EVERYWHERE

Sometime, Everywhere
I loved you.
In the darkness, in the light,
in ancient times and lives to come,
in the shadow of innumerable suns,
I loved you.

Everytime, Somewhere
alone, despaired and blind;
running in an endless night,
separated now from All That Is,
I hold for you the Vision of Bliss
as long as it takes to wake to share,
I loved you, I love you,
Every Time, Every Where.

LOVE WORDS

Love, love, I always write about love...
for can there ever be enough
love words,
expressions, affections;
written, spoken, acted?

Can there ever be enough
or too much
extolled on depths
of passion and longing?

Sentimental affirmation,
agony and elation,
which make us so exquisitely
alive yet converged
with all our selves –
such is love, love, only love.
Let's write about love.

RAVAGED

Not asking permission, he takes –
without second thoughts;
decisive, forceful; kingly, not boyish,
but graces unknown, apologies foreign;
too much to reconcile, to wrap
her narrow perspective around;
now soaked in sorrow and passion,
irreparable, irrepressible,
the heart of the savage.

No invitation, she comes –
a live hurricane
of careless opinion and presence;
demanding, exceeding all or nothing,
high expectations fulfilled, or bludgeoned;
too much to reconcile, to aspire,
from the programmed view he had;
rampant resistance afire,
so cloaked and soaked
in sorrow and passion,
these fine hearts,
ransacked and ravaged.

ACCIDENTAL LOVE

Oh accidental love,
where did you come from?
I was not asking, not expecting,
and certain, so certain
I didn't need you in my life!

Oh accidental love,
don't you always injure someone?
I was safe and content
and now broken and bent,
but these pieces create
the most beautiful of mosaics.

HOMECOMING

He aims to slip inside
like a thief in broad daylight;
his presence at the threshold
respectfully hushed,
but not at all subtle.

Surging and stretching
himself to full height;
aroused, awakened, he sighs,
and with that single breath,
breaches the darkness
and explodes into light.
She screams
in all-encompassing delight!
He has arrived.

LOVE SIMILES

I love you like the moon
loves the dark night sky;
growing ever bigger and brighter,
her illumination
the show of ages.

I love you like the rose
loves the summer sun;
his radiance deepening
her heady fragrance,
not yet to be released.

I love you like the seed
loves the warm spring earth;
cozily resting, gathering unto itself
the Creator's energy,
to burst forth at last.

I love you like I love myself
and hate myself, my childish id;
its flaws and tantrums forgiven,
as we evolve, expand, and love;
my forever, eternal love.

OUTCOMES

So outrageous sometimes
the things you say, like
"What if we had never met?"
as though that could have ever been
an outcome of this master plan;
as if the earth were flat,
or dragons were real,
or that I could stop myself
from thoughts of you
pouncing unbidden through my psyche
when asleep and awake,
relentless in my head,
and for certain it continues
long after I am dead.
So how could we have never met
when I know you live
inside of me?

BEFORE WORDS

A thousand hours spent
near each other but apart;
in blessed silence side by side,
with so few muddled words
uttered or heard;
for so many years in motion
with just gestures and expressions,
laced in simple, deep perceptions.

And although we seemed unknown
to each other's human forms,
we were hopelessly entangled
already for so long;
and such content and ease we felt
for all those early days,
until we started speaking
and the words got in the way.

VANISH

Let me drown in your essence;
plunge into that endlessly deep,
rolling river current!
Icy cold, every cell of my being tingles
and I hear, feel, and sense nothing else
except the oneness of you
enveloping my skin, my scent, my breath;
transforming me,
making the me I knew
vanish.

NOW

Make no mistake,
the worlds have conspired
to match each circumstance
of infinite time and space
for us to be together
now.

X-TOWN

My love whispers of a land
where lush, verdant mountains
touch the clouds with cold hands;
all the while, grassy feet
stick tip-toes in the sea –
Such a place, could there be?

The name rolls from his tongue,
strange sounds like singing bees
that mean nothing to me;
in a moment irretrievable,
yet this sounds unbelievable!

My mind is not convinced
this earthly place does exist,
where hills dance in salt mist;
a sandy blackness of sea,
wrapped in vivacious green
embraces like we,
and like X-town,
no one remembers our name.

I BELONG TO YOU

If I should die before my time,
let your lips meet mine,
and Anubis will recognize
that I belong to you.

A whisper, sweet breath,
and we can cheat Death!
Grab my hand, palm to palm,
lines of life pressed together;
squeeze with your passion,
and love beyond measure,
and though we may not stay
on Earth here forever,
the gods will know –
(they will know)
they are never to sever
twin spirits enjoined
in a marriage divine,
and Anubis will recognize
that now and for all of time,
I belong to you.

THE FIGHTER

THE HUMAN EXPERIENCE

CHAMPION

In your quest
to win the fight,
you are not very nice,
Champion.
Winning at all costs,
perhaps not as satisfying
as you'd thought.

For truly,
who reigns as victor
when one concedes to silence
just to end all the bicker?

Resentment still festers
and rips holes in our
nascent Resolution,
savagely slaying
the blessed babe;
a magical creature
we've never seen,
only dreamed of –
and prayed.

But savor your triumph,
as he bleeds on the floor,
for you are so deserving –
you wanted it more.

TANGLED

Her beautiful smooth surface
gave no hint of the complexity beneath;
tangled wires in intricate connections,
woven deep around and under,
twisted at times, so hopelessly nonsensical,
the most experienced professional
naught dare to give a price in time
of what it might take to put her right,
and remap this odd and twisted mess,
to make her flow and whole again.

THE FIGHT BEFORE
THE FIGHT

Such faith we have
in this body to heal!
Demanding recovery
from wretched abuse
in our quest to test
all limits of blessed corporeal.

Eyes dry and lips crack,
the heart begins to bang and thrash,
begging for escape from
this depleted trap
of drought and famine (self-inflicted),
to be in near-death moments lifted,
and then ensues a buxom climax
most complete with feast and sleep –

Only to wake to the day of war
to be physically tested yet once more,
and to suffer, recover,
and do it all over again!

RED

Red, she was,
inside and out;
fiery blood so intense,
it could melt iron
to a malleable mess.

Red, she was,
to the ends of her hair,
the length of each nail;
at times, even her eyes
flashed crimson
like full red moons
against the ominous sky
of her similarly dark soul.

Red, she was,
unpainted probing lips,
sanguine and solar-kissed;
red skin so radiant that
the deeper you probed,
the hotter her core.

Red, she was,
with saber-toothed aura;
larger than life, this inferno-cat
consumed any room;
a bubbling vortex, her physical form,
queen of this storm,
a pyro-tigress of a girl,
she was
Red.

DIKAR

(The Noble Savage)

This day of all days,
I met a noble savage.
He was a warrior I guess,
judging from his dress
and formidable demeanor,
quite intimidating, yes!
His visage, grim at best,
but when at last he spoke,
in most calm and measured tones,
I was impressed but taken back,
still suspecting an attack,
unsure if I could trust the beast –
How noble was this savage?

He said he saw for sure in me
this same inherent savagery –
Athletic prowess yet unbidden,
buried deep but not quite hidden
from him as deft and knowing
of beastly spirits locked within.

His sacred quest was now to find
those rare among us,
or not quite,
with lurking lion locked inside,
within their flesh façade of human normalcy
– this beast!

Born and bred of honor code
with every fiber, it was sewn,
each drop of blood and every cell,
knew the code and knew it well;
to teach such things
is not to tell
with complex words or pointless talk,
this beastly king just walked the walk!

I watched and begged my soul to fall
in step, to mimic such as best,
this blossoming of all the rest –
of loyalty and honor pledged
beyond the bonds of ancient kin –
of all our savage brothers.

I was initially not thrilled
with his idea of savage training;
this was suffering and straining,
so absurd and strange to me,
my human form objected loudly!
But he ordered and cajoled
the sleeping lion to the fore,
and soon my human was no more;
the savage self, unleashed at last
but what of me, what of me?

My old life no longer fit;
I was too far gone to quit
this chimeric transformation,
expert now in pain infliction,
now a wicked dereliction –
getting pleasure from the pain
I sought to give.

Resistance broken,
I was pledged
warrior-lion, perfect blend;
this day of all days
I became
a noble savage.

BOXES

Why must I check a box?
Please, yes, check a box!
For our political convenience,
it's so much easier
when things are labeled
white or black or Asian!
- Except I am not a box!
But an amalgamation
of all things human,
of all things worldly,
- and not.

Seemingly female
but perhaps today,
acting more male;
seemingly white
but perhaps inside,
colored more brown.
Anger abounds
while drawing lines
for gender and race,
creating economic, ethnic
and cultural borders,
espousing these differences,
tossing away all
that we truly are,
bound by all
of our similarities and differences.

Can we peel off
this toxic plastic wrapper
of societal pressures,
of political agendas and media frenetics
who print a label that screams
their version of us
so neatly described and designed,
so fancy and pretty...succinct?!
I will not be packaged, not be
someone's object to protest
for or against
to vilify, to glorify...not I!
I am so much more than that!
I am all those things,
all those categories,
all those boxes,
- and none.

For I,
I am me
I am you
I am us
I am not
a box.

LESSER ME

Can you not occasionally accept
the lesser version of me –
the struggling, human version of me;
the damaged, animal version of me?

And I will be grateful and accept
the lesser version of thee;
and patiently but constantly
hold tight in my eyes and heart and head
the finest version of you,
instead?

THE MATRIARCH

The matriarch was yesterday's child,
who ceremoniously shed
her cousins' hand-me-down clothes
for fine shoes and cashmere,
and buried those cousins
one at a time,
year after year,
after burying grandparents,
and uncles and aunts,
and Mother at last;
although Father lived on,
his mind was far gone,
leaving her to grasp to cling,
anticipating desperately,
further loss of fading tribe
and her the nearly next in line.

Yesterday's child adored flowers
but that odor of funerary now
makes the matriarch sick.

THE PATH

In the center of the street,
I move my feet;
rapidly, smiling,
eyes shut
yet I move quickly –
confidently, I strut.

No matter
I can't see as I stride,
for I can feel the path inside.
I caught a glimpse
only once;
just a flash
of the path
before me,
– it's enough.

Can't you see?
A glimpse is
all you need
to stride ahead,
and when you halt
and pause to breathe,
you'll be precisely where
you dreamed you'd be.

ADAM

Wicked lips that curse or kiss,
ragged nail on a fingertip,
steep chin and dimple within,
sharp angles of a jaw that flex
to corded muscles in the neck,
cradling the fruit forbidden –
rocked to sleep
when he speaks,
this divine treat,
shared after Eve took her bite,
freeing them both,
he carries it always,
suspended in the space
between heart and mind,
the telltale sign
they are two of a kind,
and reminder of whence
they had came.

SILLY FLESH WOUNDS

She was certainly, irrefutably
changed for having known him;
scars peppered her face,
crossing this way and that;
a tear duct split and stitched,
even crying was never the same.
Her nose had gained character
since they'd met,
so typically, boringly Roman
it had been.

Cracked and twisted wrist and toes;
concussions, fractured facial bones,
lips split and eyebrows glued,
so much fun they had
testing these limits,
gaping in wonder at
their superpowers to heal
these silly flesh wounds.

STUPID DRUNK

If you tried to hurt yourself
in some old-fashioned way,
other than to drink to take
your life and love away;
if you ingested arsenic,
instead of wine and beer,
could we have managed then
to fully interfere?

Could we have made a scene,
and locked you safe away?
Safe and angry and unhappy,
to live until today?
A victim of addiction,
of attempted suicide;
victim of a broken system,
mental problems so maligned.

Freedom treasured,
courts approved,
deliver liquor, paltry food;
drunk and starving tiny waif,
bleeding out and never bathed;
desperate, filthy -
ambulance;
catch and free,
it never ends.

Relentless, vicious alcohol!
Your mind and body, even soul,
no longer yours to wield control;
such like every wretched crime -
pain slowly festering in kind,
and rots you from the core inside -
a dank, molasses suicide.

Alcohol, drop by drip,
hateful now, I feel you slip;
and I am clearly not enough
for you to quit and give it up.
If it was poison-pure indeed,
could someone then have intervened?
And we could dream –
(oh, could we dream?)
that things had worked out
differently.

THE FIGHTER

In the walk of ages, he is
a Gladiator,
sequestered in the sub terrain;
pacing the pen, end to end,
focused and silent,
they wrap his hands,
hardened fists,
most precious and treasured,
to flow in perfect
pain-inflicting concert,
with the whole of his being
in measure.

Rules spoken and agreed, he is
an Apache,
riding out on the wave of his tribe;
blood brothers, side by side,
with whispers of honor and fire,
they paint his face,
bless his weapons and part ways
as he explodes into the cage,
this sacred space,
the only place
he is he–
Free.

DIADEM

No matter the time or location,
venture or occasion,
he wears a crown always now;
it never slips and perpetually shines,
weightless as iron and solid as time,
with a sole adornment gracing the brow –
a luminous lemniscate in ceaseless chase
of closing the gap in the ultimate race
to meet – or beat – Her Majesty,
Infinity.

He wears a crown always now;
the diadem a part of him,
as the calcified sabre of the mythical stallion
transforms the horse to a magical beast,
much as he can no longer be
called an ordinary man indeed.

MASTER

You are stronger but
you can't shake me;
you can yell but
you can't make me;
you can smash but
you can't break me;
you can go but
you can't take me –
for I am the only
master of my chains.

SOME WHATEVER

Here I sit
on top of my world,
not a broken, pathetic girl
crying over some whatever,
or a man who
lost his temper,
saying cruel things
to hurt, or worse –
to see myself
as something less
than the divine
feminine,
or commingled
yang to yin,
for am I not
a part of him,
himself, repackaged,
in prettier skin?

PAST LIVES

Once we were trees,
you and I -
fruit bearers with ever-changing
possibilities for growth.

Blossoms bursting,
coloring, perfuming,
creating, producing,
stretching, reaching.
Trees once more.

Once we were lions,
you and I -
ferocious twins with ever-changing
pride and purpose.

Rubbing faces,
sleeping, snuggling,
coupling, sunning,
exploring, hunting.
Lions once more.

Once we were warriors
you and I -
Thracian gladiators in ever-changing
battles of darkness and might.

Shoulders pressing,
swinging, thrusting,
bleeding, twisting,
healing, breathing.
Warriors once more.

Once we were Source
you and I –
paired spirits in ever-changing
visions of flickering light.

Chakras entwined,
floating, flying,
experiencing, vibrating,
transcending, evolving.
Source evermore.

LOST

There is nothing to say,
just an impulse one day
to paint my face
a ceremonial way;
streaks and fat lines
in red, yellow, black.
I trekked a path alone
until its end, and sat
and slashed
and watched the juice of life
leak from me;
splashing on to fallen leaves
colored now anew –
released in a moment,
released from the torment,
I swooned and sighed,
and flew.

JUST A GIRL

I am
just a girl;
a goddess, creator,
a creature, a maker,
a beast and a savior,
a coward, risk-taker,
a healer, ball-breaker,
a timekeeper, a sleeper,
a heathen, believer,
a doll, a witch,
a scratch, an itch,
a tyrant, a slave,
a mansion, a cave,
eyes brown, eyes green,
a wretched waif,
a perfect queen,
I am, I am
just
a
girl.

BEAST

Before you let me know you,
I already knew you.
I knew who you really were,
while you were still playing pretend games
in a very real fortress
of cultural mores and steel beams of shame,
protecting the good citizens
from witnessing the unthinkable –
a nurturing beast,
yet to be unleashed,
in all his femininity.

The crowds do cower,
but not I –
I dry
your tears.

THE BOY AND THE DOOR

She knew this boy
would walk with angels
and slay dragons,
or befriend them,
as wisdom suggested;
and winged feet would carry him
to stand before the Great Locked Door.

When the Graces deemed it time,
he arrived and stood alone one day;
the Great Door loomed there silently,
its peak reaching into violet sky –
grand and intimidating, it was
rigged with iron hinges, chains
and padlocks two feet thick,
bragging loudly of its dominance
through its myriad of battle scars
left by earlier crusaders;
defeated and exhausted,
they had fallen at the Door.

They had burned and battered,
pounded and pried,
at the Door, at the locks
with their tools and their might,
and the Door held,
as it had always held

secrets of time and space,
secrets to the code of soul and
where the seat of consciousness lays.

She knew this boy,
as wisdom suggested,
would regard this
ominous ogre of a Door,
draped in chains and iron locks
and ever-so-gently turn the knob.

This boy would pull with all he's got -
straight back he'd coax
his hand towards heart;
he knew this Door was never locked,
but who was he to tell them
that the locks were but a farce?
And that pushing against
never gets you what you want.

She knew this boy
with winged feet
would walk with angels
and befriend dragons,
as wisdom suggested,
knowing that the Door awaits
a simple turn and tug to open.

THE HEROINE

"All things come to an end,"
he said;
"Often with the demise
of the headstrong heroine."

She leaves behind:
the story undone –
a trove of amorous prose;
a lover, a son, most treasured
in truth,
some thought her crazy,
most thought her fun,
but none ever thought
that she would die young;
she always just had one more
last thing to say.

THE WRITER

TRANSITIONS

EARTHBOUND FOR NOW

This energy of mine,
it speaks of light divine;
of endless bounds,
loving all and both
the familiar and unknown.

Not separate but enjoined
in desperate silence of the mind,
my love is infused with all
that you have made me.

My spirit travels;
a renegade, a hanged man,
touching rounded corners,
sailing, swimming, flying;
I am resigned
to keep creating –
Earthbound for now.

THE CREATRESS

Her hand flutters,
and waves crest and tumble –
their mist rising and falling,
as rain brings the colors of life,
and love soaks his surface.

Her lips part,
and wind streams forth –
cascading and swirling,
a tornado of motion;
pure energy, focused and wild at once,
whips across his surface.

Her eyes blaze
through his mountains,
onyx canyons, obsidian seas
violated at once
by her penetrating light,
an inferno diffused, now radiant,
cradles and warms his surface.

Her voice sings;
as birds and beasts
add their sounds to the rhythm of him,
he spins and rejoices;
life abounds
on this, this playground –
his surface.

ASLEEP AWAKE

Sleepy boy, silly girl!
Close your eyes, release your mind,
breathe deep the sweet earth air.
Lay your bones, head and hair
to rest awhile, and smile
with your dream-lips, press a kiss
from your soul, awakened.
Good night and hello, my love!
How I've missed you.

TRYST

Fervid water sluiced his Adonic frame,
lasciviously lathered in fragrant foam;
so recently rubbed with the delicious,
salacious musk of her.

Now so resolutely scrubbed and rinsed,
this redolent evidence of their tryst,
released from his skin, intermingled
forever these cells, scents and juices
swirl and dilute to unfailingly end up
again and again,
down the drain.

FOR THE RIDE

She is on the move again,
changing, chasing
a grander version of herself;
so sorry she didn't warn you first
about her super-charged soul
having total control,
but she was yet unaware
that her fleshy existence,
so cared for and prized,
was simply a vehicle
employed for the ride.

MY FINAL SLEEP

Much as I am a fire child,
no fire for me, please,
for my final sleep –
to dream the dream that never ends,
to make the trip to see old friends,
to have and to hold in soothing comfort,
a silent adoration everlasting.

For my final sleep,
this lovely flesh will rest;
this formidable grand palace
was the home for my soul.
It was perfectly built and tended to
for so many years;
I loved this home.
Sometimes I even cleaned up
and invited you to visit in me;
too few minutes you'd stay,
(if you could even enter at all)
then retreat back to your own
soul's home for a sleep.

But always the better were we,
for those moments our spirits played
under one roof –
too bad we couldn't stay!
Alas, this home was all I truly had;
the only thing that was mine alone,
but you always did treasure it so

I would give it when I'm done,
except, I fear it's beyond repair;
and so when I go, it must retreat
for one final sleep
in the earth amongst rocks and trees
to vibrate with my memory,
and return to the Great All-Energy,
until my grander palace gets built
and I shall invite you again.

THAT SKIN

I see you
wrapped inside that skin;
trapped from within
that form that you scorn,
wishing to be seen as more,
to feel intrinsically adored,
as you have always been before,
as you have been evermore -
before you grew that skin.

CLOUDY ENTANGLEMENT

The wind blew clouds
across the blue.
Floating joyously, carelessly,
entangling with another
here and there,
reshaping and birthing
animal faces and figures in white,
then pulling away, yet
taking some, giving some
of what they were;
unconscious floating drifters now,
these clouds,
until they entangle again
with one another.

FOR AVA

Will you catch me
when I'm old and tired and I've had enough,
my roots no longer married to the earth,
but loosening more with every storm?

Will you catch me
when I'm ready to fly, ready to fall,
to give in, give up and jump off
from this turn of the wheel?
To lay down on the fragrant ground
until I become as one with the soil?

When the cold wind blasts
and I tremble and sway,
will you, will you,
will you catch me?

THE TREASURE

She protected her addiction like a treasure;
worthless though it was,
it came to define her.
It permeated every conscious thought
and restlessly pricked and prodded,
even during dreamless slumbers.

It was the handsome rogue who hijacked
every car, plane, train, wagon or donkey
that could take her out of this black town.
God knows she just couldn't manage on foot.
Somewhere along the way,
the rogue had even taken her shoes –
her beautiful expensive red shoes!
Now what was she to do?

Carrying the heavy treasure
was just too much to bear anymore.
It must be hidden, buried,
while she rested like so many times before.
She could lie down beside it
and perhaps the rains and winds
wouldn't cause the dirt to cover her
this time.
Or
she could damn the rogue and walk away!
Barefoot though she was...carless, assless,
her own power maybe was enough –
it had always been enough;
she didn't need that treasure anyway.
She was a queen already.

THAT PLACE

Some place away from my place
is a place unseen, undreamed;
and yet, without a doubt
I know you are there
anchoring that space,
that magical place;
resolutely keeping house
and planting gardens
here and there,
blooms and tombs everywhere;
monuments to buried lives, where
bad choices and transgressions
come to lie and be rinsed clean
by silver tears of rain,
before we come to meet you,
to greet you in that place,
that beautiful place,
where I can always see you.

YES!

She was offered this –
so fragrant and juicy,
so plump with potential
for sweetness and fullness,
completeness and just, well,
adventure!
The possibilities were endless.

Not yet ripe, but the becoming
would be glorious and fun,
and joyful and crazy and happy
and just, well,
exciting –
the growth unfathomable!

So up and down and wild,
so delightful in the
touching, tasting, smelling, seeing
each layer peeled and exalted;
so intense and delicious
it would be,
so she
said "Yes!"

ROUND TRIP

"All things come to an end"
she said, with certainty;
wondering how and when
the story would send her
over the bend and
amend her very self and
turn her outside in.

The hour was growing late and
there was still so much to do,
so much to see,
so much to become,
before coming undone
and returning once more
to the beginning.

PURPOSE

Liking what I do,
ungrateful never,
but true love lost
to some other purpose.

Latent passion,
my unique proposition,
where art thou that sets my blood afire,
and easily pours out
like torrid, fluent lava?

Effortlessly hot, racing downhill
naturally with gravity;
no plan, no choice,
until it cools
and becomes something else
entirely.

MARIGOLD MEMORIES

She thought she caught
the sultry summer scent
of yellow-orange marigolds;
and truth be told,
although she was old,
it made her feel like five years old,
and she was home again.

TREES

Waving green, it breathes
endless purification;
cleansing, healing respiration;
a gift to stave our looming,
dooming decrepitation.
Can't we just give thanks
and treasure these,
our trees?

BUTTERFLY

Don't ask what I can give,
what I can do,
what I wish I could, should,
if choices were mine
this time;
what I am,
what I have,
is a shadow of a hint –
a fleck, a speck,
tiny as a flea,
this existing me,
but oh, what could be
this possible person,
girl to be excavated,
who was once created
already but sleeping;
awoke with a kiss
and another and more;
her cocoon destroyed,
her wings employed –
beautiful, strong, but unsure
they will fly at all.

She stretches and flexes,
a colorful blur –
and is gone.

FROZEN SUNSET

Chasing it down,
westward bound
in a tin bird, so absurd
to relive the past hour
as the sun goes down,
nearly touching the ground,
lighting fire in the clouds
in blazes of orange and red,
as though Heaven itself was burning.

So strange,
it does not fade
within the hour,
and thus my eyes
relay a lie which belies
the message of the fiery
frozen sunset.

Time smiles
and dances around
relative to your here and now,
like the sun only feigning
in touching the ground,
it's just all about where
you are standing.

LATE SPRING

I have been wanting and waiting
and hoping, anticipating,
and dreaming and now
I feel your presence at last!

I was dejected, crushed and confused;
you should have come weeks ago –
before I felt so lost and scared
that the Mother herself
had gone crazy!

BLINK

Soft sounds of live guitar
drift through my bedroom,
waking me to the reality of my here and now;
that the beloved player has suddenly become
a septuagenarian, a white-bearded bard.

The once young father who deftly strummed
through the after-hours of childhood bedtimes
now rises early to play again,
this time in my home, shared with him,
as he shared with me;
the scene and the song so much the same.

The six-year-old girl falls asleep early
to the strumming downstairs
and wakes to the same,
but so much has changed –
She is now forty-eight.

THE CARDINAL AND
THE RAVEN

At some point I traded
the cardinal for the raven,
long before your own spirit
set sail on inky black wings.

Red and black pervasive hues,
since the darkness in the womb –
pierced crimson with the blood of birth,
like red-winged blackbirds caught in flight,
or woodpeckers wild in fading light,
tapping out staccato beats
in a rhythm to their redness;
quieting, eventually, as Evening cloaks
her evanescent black upon their backs.

THE SCRIBE

Just write!
When the moment strikes,
when the Heavens know,
your soul burns aglow,
your hand gives a quiver,
your spine shimmy-shivers;
then comes the command
to put pencil in hand;
a life of its own,
it scribbles away
ridiculous prose,
never seen, never known
to my own thinking cap,
I surmise I have snapped!
Who writes these words?
My self is the scribe,
yet these thoughts are not mine!
Escaping instead
from forgotten lost depths,
they bubble and burst
to my surface at first;
a vibration of mine,
for my hands to transcribe
these words that bring me
such pleasure; I boast -
that my own giddy spirit
must love writing the most!

EPILOGUE

FADE TO LIGHT

SONG OF SHAMROCKS

They jump out and call me
"Look down, look here!"
Mischievous clovers, all overgrown,
interwoven together like emerald-green snow,
each leaf disguising and hiding his brothers.
"Look down, look here!"
- a bodacious four-leaf waves and cries,
catching my eye, and I can't help but spy
the shy and timorous five-leaf
he shaded.

Emboldened now, the young ones do call;
and although I am near,
I pretend not to hear;
petting their patches, I look quite insane,
I have no time for such childish games -
searching for four-leafs,
(the Bigfoot of clovers)
but then, all at once,
their hiding was over!
I saw them suddenly, everywhere!
Dozens at once -
in my toes, in my hair!
I picked them all,
baskets at a time,
and gave them to strangers,
as though they were mine.
Every clover was welcomed
and kept as a sign,

but the magic was borrowed -
not mine, but divine!
And from this truth,
I did convince
friends to gaze down
and ask for a hint
of the glimmer of magic
a four-leaf can give;
and so, at last,
they did!

TAKE ME

Where the mountains meet the sun!
Where the river meets the sea!
There, my love, I am certain,
is the perfect place for me!

MOMMA SAID

Put your ear to the ground;
be aware of the sounds;
when it's time to go,
you will surely know
to hustle up
the buffalo,
and walk a mile
in their moccasins
before you cast
that first stone
from your glass house,
where you hide,
alone inside,
quiet as a mouse,
you dirty louse,
at least you're not
up the creek
without a paddle
this time,
my dear child.

PEOPLE PLEASERS

Please all, please none,
please yourself or come undone;
advice from many,
respect too few,
people pleasers always lose.

MIRROR, MIRROR

Mirror, mirror on the wall,
why do you exist at all?
Reflect my eyes right back at me,
to only guess what they might see;
a glimpse of image won't relay,
the whole of whom I am today.

ONE

I turn to face the sun,
as the flower has done;
yearning, wanting –
are we not the same?
One?

CRAZY, CRAZY, CRAZY

Crazy, crazy, crazy,
in a good way, they say,
like the cat chasing his tail;
joyously spinning, faster and faster,
with no goal but delight
in his dizzying pursuit;
no glorious prize,
nor innards for snacking,
just the fun, fun, fun of attacking!

Crazy, crazy, crazy,
in a good way, they say,
like me for you –
beguilement so dazzling,
with no goal but delight
in repartee and adventures,
from day until night;
no glorious prize,
nor new creature to birth,
(for we pursue only mirth!)
seeking beauty and pleasure
in each dawn new,
cause I'm crazy, crazy,
crazy for you.

BOOTS

If you cannot see the path,
you must feel the path;
but how can you feel anything at all,
when you always have your boots on?

MY FRIEND

She does not speak much
and yet I know she's happy.
She does not eat a lot
and yet I know she's full.

She does not tell me,
but yet I know she loves me.
When I think I am all by myself,
she lies here by me.

Sometime ago we met,
quite by chance at the pound.
She was so lost,
and I was there to comfort her.

So the bond was sewn;
and ever since, our love has grown.
My dog and I are friends;
she need not talk to let me know.

-Written by Donalda Narcise

MOMMY

A tiny, yellow bird
rests gently upon her shoulder.
He sings of love and peace for her;
whispering softly, she asks
the little bird to return.

The soft, yellow bird rests,
waiting patiently;
watching her as she bends and touches
even the tiniest of branches,
covering all the leaves
with a warm blanket of her love.

She waves and beckons the bird to call;
she follows;
the road is lined with the sweet smell
of delicate lavender roses.
Slowly she walks,
kissing each beautiful bloom –
following the little tiny bird,
she finally concludes
her long journey home.

-Written by Donalda Narcise

Printed in the United States
By Bookmasters